SECUNDUM COR TUUM

I08352O9

Raymond Leo Cardinal Burke

The VIRTUE *of* PATRIOTISM

Special Jubilee Edition
Including

The ENTHRONEMENT *of the* SACRED HEART *of* JESUS

The Shrine of Our Lady of Guadalupe publishes works of prayer, catechesis, and Christian reflection in service of the mission of the Shrine and the life of the Church. Rooted in pilgrimage and devotion to Our Lady of Guadalupe and her immaculate Heart, and to the Sacred Heart of Jesus, these publications seek to foster faith, deepen love for Christ, and support the faithful in living the truths of the Catholic faith.

ISBN: 978-1-963716-01-6

Learn more about the Shrine of Our Lady of Guadalupe at

guadalupeshrine.org

The Marian Catechist Apostolate is a Catholic apostolate based in La Crosse, Wisconsin, dedicated to the formation of catechists and the promotion of sound catechesis in fidelity to the Magisterium of the Church. Founded to serve the mission of evangelization and the renewal of Catholic education, the Apostolate provides programs, resources, and publications that foster a deeper knowledge of the faith and a greater love for Christ and His Church.

Portions of this book, including *The Enthronement of the Sacred Heart of Jesus* by Raymond Leo Cardinal Burke, are drawn from previously published works of the Marian Catechist Apostolate and are included here with permission.

Learn more at mariancatechist.com.

TABLE *of* CONTENTS

Prayers

Hymns

SECUNDUM COR TUUM

The VIRTUE *of* PATRIOTISM

INTRODUCTION

In every age, Holy Mother Church seeks to form her children in those virtues that safeguard the integrity of Christian life and the well-being of the earthly community in which Divine Providence has placed us. Among these virtues, there stands one of particular weight that is frequently obscured or misunderstood, especially in our time. I refer to the virtue of patriotism. It is not a merely political sentiment, nor a passing stirring of emotion, nor a partisan attachment to any program. Its roots lie in the virtue of piety by which we render due honor to God and, in Him, to those earthly bonds through which He has given us life, culture, and the first lessons in truth and goodness. In this light, patriotism belongs to the order of justice and religion. It recognizes gifts received and it orders the heart to gratitude and to duty.

Divine Providence has not fashioned us as isolated individuals who drift without origin or responsibility. He places each of us within a family and within communities. He gives us a people and a homeland whose history and traditions provide an irreplaceable sphere for moral and spiritual growth. These bonds arise from the order of Creation and they entail real obligations according to the dictates of conscience. For the Catholic, these obligations can never be separated from the demands of faith. To love one's country rightly is to acknowledge the wisdom of the Creator in the concrete circumstances of one's birth and to respond with gratitude, with generous service, and with fidelity to the moral law. Such love is purified and elevated by grace so that it is never confused with ideology or with self-interest.

Global agendas sometimes diminish the value of local belonging. Disdain for one's own cultural and historical patrimony is at times praised as if it were a virtue. In such a context, we must recover the authentic meaning of patriotism. It is, first of all, an expression of justice that acknowledges the genuine goods that our homeland has conferred upon us. It is also an expression of charity that desires the true good of our nation according to the law of God. Rightly-ordered patriotism never excuses sin and never defends injustice. Rather, it calls a people to conversion. It honors the innocent. It protects the weak. It seeks peace that is founded upon justice and truth.

The believer, therefore, loves his homeland in Christ. He brings the light of the Gospel into public life. He prays for rulers and magistrates. He pays what is due in taxes and in service. He speaks the truth with charity when laws offend the dignity of the human person or contradict the divine and natural law. He contributes to the common good through honest work and through the works of mercy. In this way, patriotism becomes a path of sanctification. It strengthens families. It purifies culture. It renews civic friendship. It disposes the earthly city to be more docile to the reign of Christ.

We must hold fast to the truth about our relationship with the land and the people who have nurtured us. We must embrace the responsibilities that arise from this bond.

We must cultivate the noble virtue of patriotism, which remains indispensable for the renewal of both Church and nation. Entrusting ourselves to Christ, who is Lord of all peoples and King of every nation, we must be resolved to fulfill our duties toward our homeland with wisdom, with gratitude, and with steadfast Christian courage. May the Most Sacred Heart of Jesus sustain our efforts. May the Immaculate Heart of Mary protect our country. May Saint Joseph watch over our families and guide us in the ways of justice and peace.

TRUTH, FILIAL PIETY, *and* PATRIOTISM[1]

Our happiness during our earthly pilgrimage and at its destination, eternal life, depends on the conformity of our daily living with the truth, that is, with the good order with which God has created and sustains the world and, in a most particular way, man and woman. Our Lord Who alone is our salvation describes Himself as "the way, and the truth, and the life."[2] He also teaches us that the truth alone will make us free: "If you continue in my word, you will truly be my disciples, and you will know the truth, and the truth will make you free."[3] He likewise describes His own vocation and mission as obedience to the will of the Father: "My food is to do the will of him who sent me, and to accomplish his work."[4]

---

[1] I have earlier published the substance of this section and the subsequent three sections: Raymond Leo Cardinal Burke, "The Truth, Filial Piety and Patriotism," *Divinitas* 59 (2016) 279-291.

[2] Jn 14, 6.

[3] Jn 8, 32.

[4] Jn 4, 34.

It is the virtue of piety, an integral part of the sevenfold gift of the Holy Spirit, which expresses our recognition of the truth and our humble obedience before the truth. Louis Bouyer provides a succinct but full description of piety:

> The gift of piety, in the Thomistic synthesis of the spiritual life, in the service of charity not only perfects the virtue of religion (seen as the form of justice toward God), but also every practice of the virtue of justice. Just as our duties toward God are raised to the highest perspective of a supernatural filial relationship, our relationships with others are transfigured in the light of the brotherly fellowship within the divine charity poured into our hearts by the Holy Spirit (cf. Rom. 5,5; see St. Thomas Aquinas, *Sum. Theol.*, Ia-IIae, q. 68, and IIa-IIae, q. 80 ff.). The virtues of filial piety and piety toward fatherland are more special; they are annexes of the virtue of justice, but the influence of the same gift gives them a specifically Christian coloring (*ibid.*, q. 101).[5]

---

[5] "Le don de piété, dans la synthèse thomiste de la vie spirituelle, perfectionne au service de la charité non seulement la vertu de religion, considérée comme la forme de la justice envers Dieu, mais tout l'exercice de la vertu de justice. Ainsi, comme nos devoirs envers Dieu sont élevés dans la perspective plus 'élevée d'un rapport filial surnaturel, nos rapports avec autrui se transfigurent dans la lumière de notre communion fraternelle à l'intérieur de la charité divine répandue dans nos cœurs par le Saint-Esprit (cf. Rom. 5, 5). Voir saint Thomas, *Sum. Theol.*, I[a] IIae, q. 68, et II[a] IIae, q. 80 ss. Plus particulières sont les vertus de piété filiale et de piété envers la patrie, annexes de la vertu de justice, mais auxquelles l'influence du même don communique une coloration spécifiquement chrétienne (Ibid., q. 101)." L. uyer, *Dictionnaire théologique* (Tournai: Desclée & Co., 1963), p. 530. English translation: Louis Bouyer, *Dictionary of Theology*, tr. Charles Underhill Quinn (New York, NY: Desclee Co., Inc., 1965), pp. 350-351.

Piety is the part of the sevenfold gift of the Holy Spirit, poured forth into our hearts from the glorious-pierced Heart of Jesus, which inspires and strengthens us to live the truth of our being as creatures created in the image and likeness of God to know, love and serve Him in this life, and to be happy forever with Him in the life which is to come.

THE MORAL ORDER *and* THE DEFENSE OF THE NATION

An essential aspect of our daily life, which pertains to the grace of piety and to the practice of the virtue of piety has to do with a truth which is called into question in our time. I refer to our relationship with our homeland, which demands of us the practice of that part of piety which is called patriotism. Before the challenges of our time, there are those who propose and work for a single global government, that is, for the elimination of individual national governments, so that all of humanity would be under the control of a single political authority.

Some quote no. 67 of the Encyclical Letter *Caritas in Veritate* of Pope Benedict XVI to claim that a form of world government is required by Catholic social teaching. Pope Benedict XVI, referring to the Encyclical Letter Pacem in Terris of Pope Saint John XXIII, writes about "an urgent need of a true *world political authority*,"[6] but he hastens to add:

---

6 "... oportet vera *Auctoritas politica mundialis* adsit." Benedictus PP. XVI, Litterae encyclicae Caritas in Veritate, "de humana integra progression in caritate veritateque," 29 Iunii 2009, *Acta Apostolicae Sedis* 101 (2009), p. 700, n. 67. [CV]. English translation: Benedict XVI, Encyclical Letter *Caritas in Veritate*, "On Integral Human Development in Charity and

> Such an authority would need to be regulated by law, to observe consistently the principles of subsidiarity and solidarity, to seek to establish the common good, and *to make a commitment to securing authentic integral human development inspired by the [goods] of charity in truth.* Furthermore, such an authority would need to be universally recognized and to be vested with the effective power to ensure security for all, regard for justice, and respect for rights.[7]

Pope Benedict XVI describes a form of international cooperation for the common good, but it cannot be said that he is advocating for one world government. The "world political authority" which he describes could only receive its mandate from the individual national governments for whose good it exists. Hence, the insistence on the principles of subsidiarity and solidarity, and on the goods of charity and truth.

At the conclusion of the text in question, he insists that "[t]he integral development of peoples and international

---

Truth," 29 June 2009 (Città del Vaticano: Libreria Editrice Vaticana, 2009), p. 110, no. 67. [CV Eng].

7 "Talis Auctoritas iure necesse est regatur, subsidiarietatis principia congruenter servet, bonum commune perficiendum curet, integram solidamque hominum progressionem sub lumine bonorum caritatis in veritate efficiat. Auctoritas sane haec ab omnibus est agnoscenda, quae reali potestate pollere debet, ut unicuique securitas, iustitiae observantia, iurium item tuitio praestentur." CV, 700-701, n. 67. English translation: CV Eng, pp. 110-111, no. 67. The English version translated the Latin word, "*bonorum*," with English word, "values," which is not felicitous, and, therefore, I have substituted the word, "goods," for the word, "values." The term, "value," which comes from the discipline of economics denotes something relative to the subject who considers it, while the term, "good," which comes from the discipline of metaphysics denotes an objective reality, independent of any subjective consideration.

cooperation require the establishment of a greater degree of international ordering, marked by subsidiarity, for the management of globalization" and "the construction of a social order that at last conforms to the moral order, to the interconnection between moral and social spheres, and to the link between politics and the economic and civil spheres."[8] The order, in general, and the moral order, in specific, to which Pope Benedict XVI refers are taught, lived and defended in the family and the homeland. As the natural law instructs us, only well-ordered and strong families and nations can provide and guarantee what is needed for a just international order for the common good. An international order, detached from the right order of families and nations, in fact, easily becomes the instrument of attacks on the most fundamental goods: the goods of life, family, and religion. It becomes one of the "other gods"[9] who, instead of safeguarding and promoting man's freedom, renders him a slave.

THE FOURTH COMMANDMENT *and* THE DUTY TO HOMELAND

For those who are convinced that the only way to achieve the common good is the concentration of all government in a single authority, loyalty to one's homeland or patriotism

---

[8] "Populorum integra progressio atque inter Nationes cooperatio secum ferunt ut internationalis quaedam altioris gradus institutio subsidiarii generis ad globalizationem moderandam condatur atque ordini morali necnon coniunctioni inter moralia et socialia, politica et oeconomica et civilia munera consentaneus socialis ordo denique constituatur." CV, 701, n. 67. English translation: CV Eng, p. 111, no. 67.

[9] Cf. Ex 20, 3.

has become an evil. It is often called nationalism, a term which evokes the evils of a misguided or corrupt national identity, obscuring the truth of our natural identity with a certain land and its culture. Already in July of 2007, the 16th Université de Renaissance Catholique devoted itself to the theme: "Le patriotisme est-il un péché?" ("Is Patriotism a Sin?")[10] Given the contemporary somewhat widespread doubt and confusion about the virtue of patriotism, it will be helpful to reflect upon what the Christian life demands of us regarding our homeland and its civil government.

The virtue of patriotism reflects excellence in the fulfillment of the demands of the Fourth Commandment of the Decalogue, the first of the last seven commandments which treat our relationships with the world and others, in accord with the primary demands of our relationship with God, which are treated in the first three Commandments. While the Fourth Commandment commands us to honor our father and mother, that is, to show to our parents the piety which flows from the recognition that they have cooperated with God in giving us the gift of human life, it also commands the piety owed to the wider community in which marriage and family become possible and indeed flourish. Saint Thomas Aquinas, in his *Summa Theologiae* teaches us:

> *I answer that,* Man becomes a debtor to other men in various ways, according to their various excellence and the various benefits received from them. On both counts God holds first

---

[10] Cf. *Le patriotisme est-il un péché ? Actes de la XVIe Université d'été de Renaissance Catholique*, Villepreux, juillet 2007 (Issy-les-Moulineaux: Contretemps, 2016).

> place, for He is supremely excellent, and is for us the first principle of being and government. In the second place, the principles of our being and government are our parents and our country, that have given us birth and nourishment. Consequently man is debtor chiefly to his parents and his country, after God. Wherefore just as it belongs to religion to give worship to God, so does it belong to piety, in the second place, to give worship to one's parents and one's country.[11]

It is clear from the Angelic Doctor's exposition that, not only is patriotism not a sin, but it is a requirement of nature itself. The term, worship (*cultus*), when applied to one's parents and one's country clearly, as Saint Thomas makes clear, is distinct from divine worship which is given to God alone. The second sense of worship is analogous and refers to the piety or devotion shown to those who cooperate with God for our good.

Reflecting upon the virtue of patriotism as an integral part of the gift and virtue of piety, in accord with the teaching

---

[11] "**Respondeo** dicendum quod homo efficitur diversimode aliis debitor secundum diversam eorum excellentiam, et diversa beneficia ab eis suscepta. In utroque autem Deus summum obtinet locum, qui et excellentissimus est, et est nobis essendi et gubernationis primum principium. Secundario vero nostri esse et gubernationis principium sunt parentes et patria, a quibus et in qua et nati et nutriti sumus. Et ideo post Deum, maxime est homo debitor parentibus et patriae. Unde sicut ad religionem pertinet cultum Deo exhibere, ita secundo gradu ad pietatem pertinet exhibere cultum parentibus et patriae." *ST* IIa IIae, q. 101, art. 1. Saint Thomas Aquinas, *Summa Theologiae Secunda Secundae, 92-189*, tr. Fr. Laurence Shapcote, OP, Volume 18 of *Latin/English Edition of the Works of St. Thomas Aquinas* (Green Bay, WI: Aquinas Institute, 2012), pp. 81-82.

of the Angelic Doctor, the *New Catholic Encyclopedia* illustrates how the practice of patriotism is a form of the charity by which we live fully the truth of our being in its relationship with God and with His Creation. The author of the entry on patriotism writes:

> But patriotism as a form of charity, or love, has a more specific object in its actuation than mankind or the human family as such. According to St. Thomas Aquinas, the particular love of one's fatherland is an important aspect of that preferential form of charity that is called *pietas* (ST 2a2ae, 101.1). Through piety the person has an obligation of love to God, parents, and fatherland. Each is in some sense a principle of man's being: God through creation; parents through procreation and education; fatherland through a formation of one's cultural and historical identity.[12]

Patriotism is an aspect of the grace of piety, which in its turn is an essential part of the grace of charity. Christ gives the grace of piety, through the outpouring of the Holy Spirit, in order that we can live the truth of our human nature.

Patriotism as such is a precept of the natural law. We see it reflected, for example, in the story of Aeneas and his father Anchises, as it is recounted by the Roman author Virgil. In fact, Virgil describes the greatness of Aeneas with the adjective, *pius*. Commenting on the *Aeneid* of Virgil and, in

---

[12] J. J. Wright, "Patriotism," *New Catholic Encyclopedia*, Vol. 10 (New York: McGraw-Hill Book Company, 1967), p. 1102. [NCE].

particular, on the excellence of the virtue of piety in Aeneas, Anthony Esolen writes:

> The name that Virgil gives Aeneas is not Odysseus' *polytropon*, the man of shifts and dodges, but the Latin word *pius*. Aeneas embodies a virtue we hardly recognize in our time: piety, which meant for the Romans a willingness to do your duty by your father and mother, your elders, your household gods, the city and state, and the great gods above.
>
> This piety is at once a deeply personal virtue and a powerful force to bring together the generations, allowing the young to take root in the soil of the old and the old to engraft their experiences onto the young, so that we sense that home is a place where the passing day partakes of long ages past and to come.[13]

Through the grace of Christ, the piety of the pagan world is elevated and perfected to be a response to God, our Creator and Redeemer, who has desired to bring us to life in Christ in the family and in a homeland. In the words of Louis Bouyer, "our relationships with others are transfigured in the light of the brotherly fellowship within the divine charity poured into our hearts by the Holy Spirit."[14]

The exposition of the Fourth Commandment in the *Catechism of the Council of Trent* or *Roman Catechism* speaks of the honor due to civil rulers, intimately connected with

---

[13] Anthony Esolen, *Nostalgia: Going Home in a Homeless World* (Washington, DC: Regnery Gateway, 2018), p. xxiii.

[14] Cf. footnote 4.

the honor due to parents and the pastors of the Church. Making reference to Saint Paul's teaching in the Letter to the Romans[15] and the First Letter to Timothy,[16] and to Saint Peter's teaching in his First Letter,[17] it underlines the truth that the honor given to civil rulers is essentially connected to the honor which we owe, above all, to God. It explains:

> For whatever honor we show them [civil rulers] is given to God, since exalted human dignity deserves respect because it is an image of the divine power, and in it we revere the providence of God who has entrusted to men the care of public affairs and who uses them as the instruments of His power.[18]

Patriotism is the recognition of the good order which God has placed in civil society, so that those who govern must respect, first and foremost, God's law, and so that those who are governed respect the civil community in which the common good is to be safeguarded and promoted.

---

15 Rom 13, 1-9.

16 1 Tm 2, 1-8.

17 1 Pt 2, 13-14.

18 "[N]am si quem eis [regibus, principibus, magistratibus, et reliquis, quorum potestati subiicimur] cultum tribuimus, is ad Deum refertur: habet enim venerationem hominum excellens dignitatis gradus, quia divinae potestatis est instar: in quo etiam Dei providentiam veneramur, qui publici muneris procurationem iis attribuit, quibusque utitur tamquam potestatis suae ministris." *Catechismus Romanus seu Catechismus ex Decreto Concilii Tridentini ad Parochos Pii Quinti Pont. Max.* iussu editus, ed. Pedro Rodríguez (Città del Vaticano: Libreria Editrice Vaticana, 1989), p. 459. [Catechismus Romanus]. English translation: *Catechism of the Council of Trent for Parish Priests*, tr. John A. McHugh and Charles J. Callan (New York: Joseph F. Wagner, Inc., 1923), p. 415. [Catechismus Romanus Eng].

The *Roman Catechism* goes on to treat the situation of wicked rulers, reminding us that the honor shown to them is not reverence toward their wrongdoing but rather toward "the authority from God which they possess."[19] At the same time, the Christian citizen must not obey their commands, if they are contrary to the moral law. The *Roman Catechism* teaches us:

> However, should their commands be wicked or unjust, they should not be obeyed, since in such a case they rule not according to their rightful authority, but according to injustice and perversity.[20]

In our time, many governments fail to or refuse to recognize that their authority comes from God, and, therefore, make laws which violate directly and grievously the moral law, for example, regarding the respect owed to all human life, from the moment of conception to the moment of natural death, regarding the integrity of human sexuality ordered to marriage and the family, and regarding the free exercise of religion itself. In many societies, there dominates an anti-life, anti-family, and anti-religious culture in open rebellion before the good order with which God has created us.

The practice of the virtue of patriotism thus faces a great challenge: the challenge to show due respect for our homeland and its government, while at the same time

---

[19] "… sed divinam auctoritatem quae in illis est." Catechismus Romanus, p. 459. English translation: Catechismus Romanus Eng p. 415.

[20] "At vero, si quid improbe, si quid inique imperent, cum id non ex potestate, sed ex iniustitia, atque animi perversitate agant, omnino non sint audiendi." Catechismus Romanus, p. 460. English translation: Catechismus Romanus Eng, p. 416.

refusing to comply with unjust laws. Here it is important to note the witness of numerous faithful individuals and families who heroically live the faith without compromise in totally secularized cultures. Before evil laws and the pressures of a totally secularized culture, they follow the example of Saint Peter and the Apostles who, when they were brought before the high priest, demanding that they deny Christ and His teaching, replied: "We must obey God rather than men."[21] The Christian citizen must frequently fulfill the demands of patriotism today by martyrdom, which is often white but sometimes red. His witness to the truth of the moral law regularly meets with the white martyrdom of indifference, ridicule and persecution, and even, in some circumstance, with the red martyrdom of death.

The *Catechism of the Catholic Church* promulgated by Pope Saint John Paul II on August 15, 1997, in its treatment of the Fourth Commandment, contains a lengthy exposition on the duties of civil authorities and of citizens. It makes clear that the authority which the civil government exercises comes from God and must respect the law which He has written in nature. It declares:

> The exercise of authority is measured morally in terms of its divine origin, its reasonable nature and its specific object. No one can command or establish what is contrary to the dignity of persons and the natural law.[22]

---

21 Acts 5, 29.

22 "Auctoritatis exercitium eius origine divina, eius natura rationali et eius obiecto specifico moraliter regulatur. Nemo potest id praecipere vel instituere, quod personarum dignitati et legi naturali est contrarium." *Catechismus Catholicae Ecclesiae* (Città del Vaticano: Libreria Editrice Vaticana, 1997), n. 2235. [CCC]. English translation: *Catechism of the Catholic Church*, 2nd ed. (Città del Vaticano: Libreria Editrice Vaticana, 1997), no. 2235. [CCC Eng].

THE DUTIES OF CITIZENS IN THE ORDER OF CHARITY

The *Catechism* goes on to explain that the exercise of authority in civil society must respect the God-given rights of the individual and, therefore, should safeguard and promote the common good.[23]

Regarding the duties of citizens, the *Catechism of the Catholic Church* repeats the constant teaching of the Church which requires that "[t]hose subject to authority should regard those in authority as representatives of God, who has made them stewards of his gifts."[24] It reminds us that "[t]he love and service of one's country follow from the duty of gratitude and belong to the order of charity,"[25] specifying the moral obligation "to pay taxes, to exercise the right to vote, and to defend one's country."[26]

The *Catechism of the Catholic Church* then takes up the obligations of "more prosperous nations … , to the extent that they are able, to welcome the foreigner in search of the security and the means of livelihood which he cannot find in his country of origin."[27] Such welcome, as is clear from the text, is not indiscriminate, for it depends on the capacity

---

23 Cf. CCC, n. 2237.

24 "… [i]lli, qui autoritati sunt subiecti, suos aspiceitn superiores tamquam repraesentantes Dei qui eos ministros Suorum instituit donorum." CCC, n. 2238. English translation: CCC Eng, no. 2238.

25 "Amor et servitium *patriae* ex officio oriuntur gratitudinis et ex ordine caritatis." CCC, n. 2239. English translation: CCC Eng, no. 2239.

26 "… tributorum solutionem, exercitium iuris suffragii, defensionem nationis." CCC, n. 2240. English translation: CCC Eng, no. 2240.

27 "… [n]ationes ditiores …, in quantum fieri potest, alienigenam, qui securitatem quaerit et opes necessarias pro vita, quas in sua originis regione nequit invenire." CCC, n. 2241. English translation: CCC Eng, no. 2241.

of nations to accept such refugees from their homelands and on the impossibility of the refugees to find the means to live in their homelands.

The paragraph goes on to specify that "[p]olitical authorities, for the sake of the common good for which they are responsible, may make the exercise of the right to immigrate subject to various juridical conditions, especially with regard to the immigrants' duties toward their country of adoption."[28] The *Catechism* further underlines the obligation of immigrants "to respect with gratitude the material and spiritual heritage of the country that receives them, to obey its laws and to assist in carrying civic burdens."[29]

The *Catechism* then repeats the perennial teaching of the Church regarding a citizen's obligation in conscience "not to follow the directives of civil authorities when they are contrary to the demands of the moral order, to the fundamental rights of persons or the teachings of the Gospel."[30] It should be noted that the rights of persons in question are those rights inherent to the God-given moral order, not the many so-called rights, for example, the right to define life and death, and the right to define sexual identity and marriage, which have been invented by man

---

28 "… [p]oliticae auctoritates possunt ratione boni communis, cuius suscipiunt munus, exercitium iuris emigrationis diversis condicionibus subiicere iuridicis, praesertim observantiae officiorum emigrantis erga nationem adoptionis." CCC, n. 2241. English translation: CCC Eng, no. 2241.

29 "… cum gratitudine patrimonium observare materiale et spirituale nationis eum accipientis, eius oboedire legibus et ad eius conferre onera." CCC, n. 2241. English translation: CCC Eng, no. 2241.

30 "… ne praescriptiones auctoritatum civilium sequatur, cum haec praecepta exigentiis ordinis moralis, iuribus fundamentalibus personarum vel doctrinis Evangelii contraria sunt." CCC, n. 2242. English translation: CCC Eng, no. 2242.

in our time. In accord with the perennial moral teaching, resistance to unjust laws of a state does not permit a refusal to carry out one's fundamental duties toward the state.[31]

The *Catechism* also spells out the moral requirements for a legitimate "[a]rmed *resistance* to oppression by political authority."[32] Five conditions are given for legitimate armed resistance before an unjust political authority: "1) there is certain, grave, and prolonged violation of fundamental rights; 2) all other means of redress have been exhausted; 3) such resistance will not provoke worse disorders; 4) there is well-founded hope of success; and 5) it is impossible reasonably to foresee any better solution."[33] Clearly, the Christian citizen is obliged to be steadfastly involved in fostering a just and charitable society. Such engagement may lead, in situations which meet all of the necessary conditions, to the use of resistance, in order to exercise faithfully the virtue of patriotism.

Finally, the *Catechism of the Catholic Church* takes up the situation of most states in our time, whose philosophical foundations and modus operandi are totally secular, that is, of states that do not recognize "man's origin and destiny in God, the Creator and Redeemer."[34] Quoting the teaching of the Second Vatican Ecumenical Council, the

---

[31] Cf. CCC, n. 2242.

[32] "... [a]ctio resistendi oppressionis potestatis politicae ad arma." CCC, n. 2243. English translation: CCC Eng, no. 2243.

[33] "... 1. in casu in quo certo, graviter et continuo iura violantur fundamentalia; 2. postquam omnes alii recursus exhausti sunt; 3. dummodo ne peiores provocenter inordinationes; 4. cum spes fundata habetur prosperi exitus; 5. si impossibile est meliores solutiones rationabiliter praevidere." CCC 2243. English translation: CCC Eng, no. 2243.

[34] "... in Deo, Creatore et Redemptore, originem et destinationem hominis." CCC, n. 2244. English translation: CCC Eng, no. 2244.

Catechism indicates that the refusal to recognize and obey an objective order of things leads to a totalitarian state, as history sadly illustrates. The Church, therefore, does not confuse herself with the political community, in accord with Our Lord's own teaching in the Gospel,[35] but exercises her responsibility to be "both the sign and the safeguard of the transcendent character of the human person."[36] In that regard, the *Catechism* repeats the perennial teaching of the Church, set forth in the Pastoral Constitution Gaudium et Spes of the Second Vatican Council: "It is part of the Church's mission 'to pass judgments even in matters related to politics, whenever the fundamental rights of man or the salvation of the soul requires it'."[37]

Patriotism teaches us to recognize our natural condition as members of a family and citizens of a homeland. Our personal identity comes principally from the family but also, and indeed because the family thrives only in wider society, from our homeland. That natural condition defines our rights and duties as a citizen. It is clear that we and our homelands have responsibilities within the international community, but those responsibilities can only be fulfilled through a sound life in the family and in the homeland. Patriotism, in fact, fosters the virtue of charity which clearly embraces citizens of other nations, recognizing and

---

35 Cf. Mt 22, 15-22; Mk 12, 13-17; and Lk 20, 19-26.

36 "... simul signum est et tutamentuum transcendentiae personae humanae." CCC, n. 2245. English translation: CCC Eng, no. 2245. Cf. Concilium Oecumenicum Vaticanum Secundum, Constitutio Pastoralis Gaudium et Spes, n. 76.

37 "Ad missionem pertinent Ecclesiae «iudicium morale ferre, etiam de rebus quae ad ordinem politicum respiciunt, quando personae iura fundamentalia aut animarum salus id exigant, ...»." CCC, n. 2246. English translation: CCC Eng, no. 2246.

respecting their distinct cultural and historical identity.[38] Such charity is fostered by the Church's exercise of her moral authority, not assuming the role of Caesar but insisting that Caesar obey the divine authority which makes legitimate and just his governance. The divine authority, in accord with the order written upon the human heart, does not make just and legitimate a single global government. In fact, the divine law illumines our minds and hearts to see that such a government would be, by definition, totalitarian, assuming the divine authority over the governance of the world. Not without reason, the sinful pride which would inspire the pursuit of a single global government has been likened to the pride of our ancient ancestors, after the Deluge, who thought that they could unite heaven with earth by their forces alone, building the Tower of Babel.[39] On the contrary, God meets us and orders our lives for the good in the family and in the homeland.

---

[38] Cf. NCE, p. 1102.

[39] Cf. Gn 11, 1-9. The English philosopher and political theorist Michael Oakshott developed the comparison of contemporary political ideologies with the story of the Tower of Babel in two essays: Michael Oakshott, "The Tower of Babel," in *Rationalism in politics and other essays*, new and expanded edition (Indianapolis, IN: Liberty Fund, 1991), pp. 465-487, and "The Tower of Babel," in *On History and Other Essays* (Indianapolis, IN: Liberty Fund, 1999), pp. 179-210. Without entering into a critical analysis of the philosophical presuppositions of Oakshott's theory, it is helpful to note what he identifies as a kind of self-defined "perfectionism," abstracted from the objective good of man, which, while proposing to pursue the common good, works against it. Elizabeth Corey comments on Oakshott's reading of the contemporary situation in terms of the Tower of Babel: "Whether one wants to contribute to a great and noble cause or to change the world through human action, pride and overestimation lie at the center of this myth." Elizabeth Corey, "The Religious Sensibility of Michael Oakshott" in *A Companion to Michael Oakshott*, ed. Paul Franco and Leslie Marsh (University Park, PA: The Pennsylvania State University Press, 2012), p. 139.

CONCLUDING THOUGHTS

In the face of the profound confusion of our time, it is essential that we remain steadfast in the truth about God's ordering of creation and, in particular, about the natural and grace-filled bonds that unite us to our families and to our homeland. These are not accidental or merely cultural arrangements, nor are they subject to the shifting winds of personal preference or political fashion. Rather, they are manifestations of Divine Providence, by which the Lord forms us, protects us, and prepares us to take up our responsibilities within the Church and within the civil community. To honor these bonds with integrity is to practice the virtue of piety, that foundational aspect of justice by which we render to God, to our parents, and to our country what is rightly owed to them. In this way, our lives are ordered according to the justice and charity that flow from the Sacred Heart of Christ.

True patriotism, then, is not an ideology nor a merely emotional attachment to one's land, but a virtue—an expression of gratitude to Almighty God for the many goods we have received through our homeland, for the faith transmitted to us, for the sacrifices of our forebears, and for the order that makes possible the flourishing of family and society. It is the willingness to labor generously for our country's true good in accord with the moral law. Authentic patriotism resists every attempt to dissolve the identity of nations or to subject peoples to systems of power detached from the natural law and from the sovereignty of God. It opposes ideologies that disregard the dignity of the human person or undermine the family as the first cell of society. It seeks instead to strengthen the domestic Church, to foster social harmony, and to defend the freedom of the Church to carry out her divine mission for the salvation of souls.

Let us, therefore, embrace with renewed courage the duties that arise from our love for God, for our families, and for our homeland. Fidelity to these divinely established bonds requires both discernment and sacrifice, especially in a culture increasingly forgetful of God and hostile to His law. Entrusting ourselves to the intercession of the Blessed Virgin Mary, Queen of Heaven and Patroness of our nation, may we work with confidence for the restoration of right order in our homes and in society. May we labor with unwavering hope so that Christ the King may reign fully in our hearts and in the life of our beloved country, guiding her along the path of truth, justice, and authentic peace.

SECUNDUM COR TUUM

The ENTHRONEMENT *of the* SACRED HEART *of* JESUS

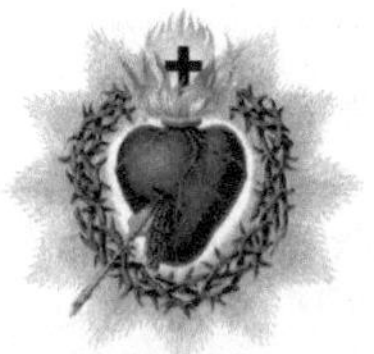

DEVOTION *to the* SACRED HEART OF JESUS

INTRODUCTION

Devotion to the Sacred Heart of Jesus is a most effective means of living always in the company of Our Lord Jesus Whom we receive in Holy Communion. Our devotion to the Sacred Heart of Jesus is an extended act of love for Him Who shows us the greatest possible love by offering His Body and Blood for us in the Eucharistic Sacrifice. In His fourth apparition to Saint Margaret Mary Alacoque, Our Lord revealed His Sacred Heart, declaring:

"Behold this Heart which has so loved men that It spared nothing, even going so far as to exhaust and consume Itself, to prove to them Its love. And in return I receive from the greater part of men nothing but ingratitude, by the contempt, irreverence, sacrileges and coldness with which they treat Me in this Sacrament of Love. But what is still more painful to Me is that even souls consecrated to Me are acting in this way."[40]

---

[40] Louis Verheylezoon, S.J., *Devotion to the Sacred Heart* (The Newman Press, 1955), xxvii; cf. Margaret Mary Alacoque, *The Autobiography of St. Margaret Mary* (TAN, 1986), 106-107.

When the devotional life is neglected, there follows a loss of gratitude and reverence, and a coldness before Our Lord in the Eucharist. Our Lord asked Saint Margaret Mary to make known His desire for a renewed devotion to His Sacred Heart so that He might give His love ever more abundantly, and that we might respond with gratitude and return love for His divine love. Devotion to the Sacred Heart of Jesus consists of an ardent love for Jesus Christ in the Holy Eucharist with grief at seeing Him so little honored and with acts of reparation for the contempt and offenses committed against Him.

THE CENTER OF DEVOTION TO THE SACRED HEART

The center of devotion to the Sacred Heart of Jesus is the Enthronement of an image of the Sacred Heart in the home. The enthroned image of the Sacred Heart, which may be a picture or a statue, expresses Christ's true Kingship, daily reminding each member of the family to follow in His royal way by making reparation for sins committed and by striving to serve God and neighbor more lovingly.

By the Enthronement of the Sacred Heart, we link the tabernacle of our parish church to our home, inviting Our Lord to be our constant and most intimate Companion. The Enthronement is a way of life. It means that Christ is King of our hearts, and that we desire Him to be present with us always. By the Enthronement, we signify our desire to make our hearts and our homes holy, to sanctify our lives in every aspect.

THE ENTHRONEMENT *and* SINGLE PERSONS

Here it should be noted that the Enthronement can be made in every home. Often, in speaking of the Enthronement, I refer to the family, but it is understood that the home may be of a single person. The person living alone, no less than a family household, rightly desires that Christ be his or her constant Companion. Also, there is always a relationship with others (family, friends, colleagues and co-workers) which is expressed in the Enthronement, even by the person who lives alone.

THE ENTHRONEMENT *and* THE TRANSFORMATION OF SOCIETY

The practice of the Enthronement of the Sacred Heart of Jesus in the home was begun by Father Mateo Crawley-Boevey, SS.CC. (1875-1961), the great *Apostle of the Enthronement*. Father Crawley-Boevey's work was first confirmed and blessed by Pope Saint Pius X in 1907, and then by every Pope since. When the Holy Father heard of the Enthronement, he told Father Crawley-Boevey directly: "To save the family is to save society. The work you are undertaking is a work of social salvation. Consecrate your life to it."[41] Father Crawley-Boevey could not mistake the importance which the Holy Father gave to his Apostolate.

Father Crawley-Boevey insisted on the *official* and *social* recognition of the rule of the Sacred Heart of Jesus

---

[41] cf. Mateo Crawley-Boevey. *Jesus, King of Love* (Paraclete Press, 1997), 1-3.

over the Christian family. The Enthronement is social because Christ's Kingship involves every member of the household in which we live and all our relationships with others, inside and outside the home. Those who carry out the Enthronement inevitably comment on the difference it makes in the relationships of family members with each other and with others.

The Enthronement is also official, in so far as it is the outward expression of an interior commitment to submit one's whole life in obedience to Christ. It is an expression of our acceptance of Him as King of our hearts, and as our constant Companion and Friend. By means of the Enthronement, the grace of the Eucharist extends into the Christian home and, from the Christian home, to the whole world, so that what the saintly Roman Pontiff declared to Father Crawley-Boevey in 1907 remains true in our time. If the company of Christ is cultivated in our homes, His company will be cultivated in every sector of life for the transformation of our society and our world into a civilization of love.

THE ENTHRONEMENT *and* CONSECRATION

The Enthronement includes necessarily our Consecration to the Sacred Heart of Jesus. The Enthronement without the Consecration would simply amount to the placing of a sacred image in a prominent place in the home. It would be a good and pious practice, but it would not transform lives in the way that the Enthronement, together with the Consecration, does. The Consecration is a "setting apart," a formal dedication of oneself to the Sacred Heart of Jesus. It involves a total offering of oneself to Him, along with the promise of fidelity in the future.

The *Act of Consecration*[42] gives expression to the profound meaning of enthroning the image of the Sacred Heart in the home. By the words of Consecration, we articulate the meaning of the Enthronement. We place our hearts totally into the Sacred Heart of Jesus, and we beg Him to be the source of our healing and strength, the medicine and nourishment by which our poor and wounded hearts are made strong and whole. The enthroned image of the Sacred Heart gives us the occasion to renew frequently, throughout the day, our *Act of Consecration.*

The words of the *Act of Consecration* proclaim the reign of the Sacred Heart of Jesus in the heart of each member of the household and in the home itself. The words express the commitment of the family members to return love to the Sacred Heart of Jesus in response to the constant and immeasurable love which He shows us in and through His Church. The *Act of Consecration* pledges frequent reception of Holy Communion, penance for sins committed and acceptance of the Divine Will at death. In short, it is a full response to the twelve promises given by Our Lord to Saint Margaret Mary.[43]

[42] See page 85 for the *Act of Consecration of the Family*, or page 129 for the *Act of Consecration in Parishes, Catholic Schools, and Other Settings.*
[43] See page 35.

THE ENTHRONEMENT *and* THE IMMACULATE HEART OF MARY

The Consecration to the Sacred Heart of Jesus is made through the Immaculate Heart of Mary, for the Blessed Virgin Mary remains for us always our Advocate before God, and the Mediatrix of the abundant outpouring of His grace from the Heart of Jesus. Since the Enthronement is made in accord with her maternal example and through her intercession, it is altogether fitting that the faithful consecrate themselves to the Immaculate Heart of Mary and install her image at the time of the Enthronement of the Sacred Heart of Jesus. As the Mother of God stood faithfully at the foot of the Cross, permitting her Immaculate Heart to be spiritually pierced because of her total union with the Sacred Heart of Jesus, so she draws us to enthrone the image of the Sacred Heart in our homes and to consecrate our hearts, one with her Immaculate Heart, to the Sacred Heart of her Son.

Raymond Leo Cardinal Burke

SECUNDUM COR TUUM

SUMMARY OF THE PROMISES OF THE SACRED HEART

Our Lord made the following twelve promises to Saint Margaret Mary Alacoque for those who honor His Sacred Heart:

1. I will give them all the graces necessary for their state of life.
2. I will give peace in their families.
3. I will console them in all their troubles.
4. They shall find in My Heart an assured refuge during life and especially at the hour of death.
5. I will pour abundant blessings on all their undertakings.
6. Sinners shall find in My Heart the source and infinite ocean of mercy.
7. Tepid souls shall become fervent.
8. Fervent souls shall speedily rise to great perfection.
9. I will bless the homes in which the image of My Sacred Heart shall be exposed and honored.
10. I will give to priests the power to touch the most hardened hearts.
11. Those who propagate this devotion shall have their name written in My Heart, and it shall never be effaced.
12. The all-powerful love of My Heart will grant to all those who shall receive Holy Communion on the First Friday of nine consecutive months the grace of final repentance; they shall not die under My displeasure, nor without receiving their Sacraments; My Heart shall be their assured refuge at that last hour.

The ENTHRONEMENT *of the* SACRED HEART *of* JESUS

The Enthronement of the Sacred Heart of Jesus is a devotional practice wherein an image of the Sacred Heart is enthroned in a prominent place in the home. It is also praiseworthy when carried out in a church, school, business or other area of human activity. The Enthronement, along with the Consecration to the Sacred Heart of Jesus through the Immaculate Heart of Mary, publicly proclaims the rule of the Heart of Jesus over the persons and activities of the place. It is an act of reparation for offenses committed against His Heart and, by the *Act of Consecration*, a pledge to honor the Sacred Heart now and in the future.

UNDERSTANDING THE ENTHRONEMENT

The Enthronement of the visible image of Our Lord represents our interior commitment to love and obey Him. In his book, *Jesus King of Love*, Father Mateo Crawley-Boevey helps us to understand the Enthronement: "By means of the Enthronement, Jesus really enters the home to have a part in and guide the whole life of the family. His love becomes the soul of both parents and children and His Heart their shrine."[44]

"In the home which acclaims the Heart of Jesus as its King of Love, the Enthronement ought to be the beginning of a *new life*, far more intimate in faith and much more ardent in charity.... This means sharing our family life with Jesus to Whom a throne has been offered precisely in order that He may remain and abide with His friends, blessing everything in the house from dawn to twilight and from the cradle to the grave. How much easier it is to live and struggle, to keep a bright face in spite of our sorrows, when Jesus is the center of the beloved home, when He presides over it as a Friend, Confidant and King. Everything is ennobled and sanctified in this enviable Bethany because Jesus shares the family joys and sorrows. *He really lives* in such a home, and the family lives by Him and with Him."[45]

---

[44] Francis Larkin, *Enthronement of the Sacred Heart* (National Sacred Heart Enthronement Center, 2009), 130.
[45] Larkin, *Enthronement of the Sacred Heart*, 141.

BLESSINGS FROM THE ENTHRONEMENT

When we wholeheartedly invite Jesus into our homes and enthrone Him as our faithful Friend and loving King, the true Head of our family, we receive many blessings. Father Crawley-Boevey explains that, "when Jesus crosses the threshold of your home He will say to you, 'Peace be to this house and to all who dwell therein.' Because you have carried out His divine request to be invited to your home, He keeps His promise to bless your family and all its undertakings, to sanctify your joys and sorrows, to console you in all your trials, to keep your family united and to give to it true peace and happiness."[46]

LIVING THE ENTHRONEMENT *and* CONSECRATION

Father Francis Larkin, SS.CC., who succeeded Father Crawley-Boevey in the promotion of the Enthronement of the Sacred Heart of Jesus, describes what it means to live daily the Consecration to the Sacred Heart of Jesus and to express the Kingship of Christ in our hearts and in our homes. In his book, *Enthronement of the Sacred Heart*, Father Larkin explains that, by the acts of Enthronement and Consecration, the family is saying, in effect, "Lord, we want You to rule over our family; we adore You as our King of Love; we accept You as our loving Friend, always occupying the first place in our hearts and in our home."[47]

---

[46] Larkin, *Enthronement of the Sacred Heart*, 136.
[47] Larkin, *Enthronement of the Sacred Heart*, 65.

The image of the Sacred Heart visibly represents the Headship of Jesus in the home; the place of enthronement becomes the "holy place" where we gather for daily prayer or whenever help is needed. Jesus is present in our home with us; He is our constant Friend and Guest, ready to help us at any moment. Indeed, He has promised that, "where two or three are gathered in My name, there am I in the midst of them."[48]

The two most important aspects of the Enthronement are Christ's *Kingship* and His *Friendship*. As King and Head of the home, Christ takes His rightful place of authority. He guides and watches over everyone and over every activity. The father, who is head of his family, turns to Christ for wisdom and guidance in making the best decisions as he strives to meet the needs of his children, support his wife, and love all who visit the home. With great humility, he welcomes Christ as Head of his family, the *domestic Church*. As a loyal subject of Jesus, he leads his family in prayer, frequent reception of the Sacraments and faithfully following the laws of the Church. The mother, like Mary, also turns to Christ as Head. In a spirit of humility and obedience, she asks Christ for the grace to be a good wife and for the grace to guide her children so that they may grow in holiness. As a result, the children learn to turn to Christ, asking for the grace they need to be obedient to their parents and to live in conformity with His will. Children growing up in a home that witnesses to Christ as the center and King of the family will naturally carry Christ's Kingship into their own future families.

---

[48] Matthew 18:20.

GROWING IN LOVE FOR THE SACRED HEART

Our Lord showed Saint Margaret Mary His Heart as a sign of the great love He has for us. He said to her, "Behold this Heart which has loved men so much." When we see His Heart, we are to be reminded that God is love, and that He desires our love in return. While enthroning the Sacred Heart and keeping His Commandments publicly acknowledges His Kingship and Headship, striving to love Him more and more each day is necessary if we are to preserve and deepen our friendship with Him. Frequent participation in the Holy Sacrifice of the Mass and the worthy reception of our King in the Holy Eucharist are particularly fruitful means of deepening our love for and friendship with Christ.

Praying together as a family, sharing with Him the joys and sorrows which form the common experience of all families, and turning to Christ frequently throughout the course of the day to offer little aspirations such as "Sacred Heart of Jesus, I love You" or "Sacred Heart of Jesus, I trust You" help to renew our zeal for living a life for Christ. *The Daily Prayer to the Sacred Heart of Jesus* is in itself a renewal of one's Consecration. Many families choose to pray this prayer together at some point during the day; for example, each night at mealtime or after praying the family rosary. It is important, however, to renew periodically the *Act of Consecration* on First Fridays, on special days such as anniversaries or birthdays, or even during times of sickness or death.

Living the Enthronement and Consecration to the Sacred Heart of Jesus is a generous and fitting response to His great love for us. In this way, we continually welcome Christ as King, Friend and true Head of the home.

The following practices help us to live a life of love with the Sacred Heart:

1. **Morning Offering** – daily offering our prayers, works, joys and sufferings to Christ;[49]
2. **Daily Prayer to the Sacred Heart** – daily renewing our pledge of love and loyalty to Christ the King;[50]
3. **Holy Rosary** – daily praying at least one decade, expressing devotion to our Blessed Mother, who unites our prayers to hers, and whose intercession thereby renders our prayers more effective;[51]
4. **Conversation with Our Lord** – turning frequently to the Sacred Heart in prayer, speaking with Him throughout each day and offering such aspirations as *Sacred Heart of Jesus, have mercy on me; Heart of Jesus, help me to love You more and more*;
5. **Reading of the Gospels** – daily meditation on the Gospels whereby we become immersed in the life of Christ and come to know His love for us;
6. **Acts of Reparation** – making acts of love in reparation to the Sacred Heart of Jesus for injuries done to Him by the sins of mankind.[52]

---

[49] See page 149.

[50] See page 150.

[51] See page 152.

[52] Reparation is necessary to satisfy divine justice. The foremost act of reparation, the only perfect one, is the Holy Sacrifice of the Mass. Other forms of reparation include making Holy Hours and offering our daily trials and sufferings in a spirit of penance and sacrifice to Our Lord.

7. **Holy Sacrifice of the Mass** – frequent, even daily, participation when possible by at least one member of the family, particularly on the First Friday of every month, in accord with Our Lord's twelfth promise to Saint Margaret Mary Alacoque;[53]

8. **Regular Holy Hours** – visiting the Blessed Sacrament for adoration in order to develop a great love for and devotion to the Real Presence of Jesus in the Holy Eucharist. If possible, making a Holy Hour at home or in a church on the Thursday night before First Friday in reparation to Our Lord according to His instruction to Saint Margaret Mary Alacoque: "'it was My will to suffer in the Garden of Olives…To join with Me in this humble prayer which I then offered to My Father, you shall rise between eleven o'clock and midnight; you shall prostrate yourself with Me for one hour… both to appease the anger of God by imploring mercy for sinners, and to sweeten in some way the bitterness I felt when My Apostles abandoned Me, being unable to watch one hour with Me.' The generous sacrifice of an hour of one's sleep is richly rewarded, not only by remarkable conversions, especially in one's own family, but also by an increase of love for the Sacred Heart of Jesus."[54] Father Crawley-Boevey provides meditations for these Holy Hours in his book, Holy Hours.

---

[53] See page 35.
[54] Larkin, *Enthronement of the Sacred Heart*, 37.

9. **First Fridays and the Feast of the Sacred Heart** (which falls on the Friday after the Solemnity of Corpus Christi) – making it a family tradition to attend Holy Mass, and praying the *Act of Consecration*[55] or the *Act of Renewal*[56] in reparation for the lack of love for Christ in the Holy Eucharist;

10. **Promotion of the Enthronement and Consecration** – making the Sacred Heart of Jesus better known and loved, most especially by the loving witness of our lives.

[55] See page 85 for the *Act of Consecration of the Family*, or page 129 for the *Act of Consecration in Parishes, Catholic Schools, and Other Settings.*
[56] See page 151.

PREPARATION *for the* ENTHRONEMENT

THE NECESSITY OF PREPARATION

Anytime we are about to undertake an important action, we give ourselves ample time to prepare. Certainly, when we desire to consecrate ourselves to Christ, we want to prepare well. It would be a mockery of the worst sort to enthrone the image of the Sacred Heart of Jesus thoughtlessly, without regard for the profound meaning of our action. It would be a demonstration of the lack of reverence and the coldness toward Our Lord to which He referred in His fourth apparition to Saint Margaret Mary.[57]

Since the Enthronement is a way of life for us, demanding our daily conversion of heart, we do not undertake it without considering carefully what it means for us. Our preparation should deepen in us our understanding and our desire for the Enthronement and Consecration.

---

[57] cf. Verheylezoon, *Devotion to the Sacred Heart*, xxvii.

The preparation has three principal parts: study, prayer and practical arrangements. Each part is important to the proper disposition of those involved. The goal of the preparation is hearts aflame with love for Christ. Only careful preparation and a thoughtful Act of Enthronement and Consecration will dispose minds and hearts to follow Christ the King, to trust in His never-failing love and to place our hearts into His.

PREPARING BY STUDY

The first important means of preparation is study. Study deepens our knowledge of the Enthronement and its meaning for our daily living. Father Mateo Crawley-Boevey has provided a complete presentation on the Enthronement and Consecration in his book, *Jesus King of Love*. Father Francis Larkin, of the same religious community as Father Crawley-Boevey, has also written an excellent book on the various aspects of the Enthronement entitled *Enthronement of the Sacred Heart*. Both books are highly recommended.

PREPARING BY PRAYER

Before the image of the Sacred Heart is enthroned in a special place, we should prepare ourselves spiritually; the second means of preparation is prayer. Father Crawley-Boevey has suggested special prayers on each of the three days which immediately precede the day of Enthronement. This three-day period of prayer, called a *triduum*, can easily be adapted for use by any group and may include other special prayers and acts of charity.

Each day of the *Triduum of Prayers* includes a meditation on a mystery of Jesus' life as presented in Sacred Scripture, one decade of the Rosary, the *Litany of the Sacred Heart* and prayers to help prepare us for the outpouring of grace we will receive by consecrating ourselves to the Heart of Jesus.

Participation in the Holy Sacrifice of the Mass and reception of Holy Communion on each day of the triduum is highly recommended and is particularly fitting for all involved on the day of Enthronement.

The *Triduum of Prayers* begins on page 51 for Enthronement in the home, and on page 93 for Enthronement in other settings.

PRACTICAL ARRANGEMENTS FOR ENTHRONEMENT OF THE SACRED HEART

The place of the Enthronement (whether in the home, parish, school or other setting) must be fitting. In other words, it should be a central place, a place in which family or members of the community spend time each day. The living room, for example, is often the best place for the Enthronement in the home.

The image of the Sacred Heart may be enthroned on a small table upon which flowers, candles, a Bible, prayer intentions and pictures of absent loved ones or those in need of prayer can be placed. If the image is hung on a wall, a small shelf should be placed under it for the same objects. In any case, the place of Enthronement should reflect the great reverence and love which we have for Our Lord. It should be the most dignified and beautiful place in the room.

On the day of Enthronement, a separate table for the image and holy water should be set in a different room, or at least a different part of the room. The image will be carried from this table to its place of permanent Enthronement.

The Enthronement is fittingly led by a priest, if possible, but can also be led by a deacon, the head of the household, principal of the Catholic school, or other appropriate figure of authority.

Invite family and friends to the Rite of Enthronement. The invitation gives a strong witness to the Catholic faith and its practice, and has the potential of inspiring others to learn about the Enthronement, and eventually to enthrone the image of the Sacred Heart of Jesus in their own homes. Copies of the Enthronement Ceremony should be available for all who are invited so that they may participate as fully as possible.

Finally, it would be good to have some refreshments after the Enthronement so that all present can continue to express their joy on this grace-filled day of Enthronement and Consecration. The social time provides an excellent opportunity to explain to others the beauty of the Enthronement. It is a natural time to give witness to our love of the Sacred Heart of Jesus.

List of supplies:

- Image of the Sacred Heart of Jesus Holy Water
- Bible Candles
- Copies of the Enthronement Ceremony

TRIDUUM *of* PRAYERS *for the* ENTHRONEMENT IN THE HOME

THE FIRST DAY

To the Heart of Our King, Jesus of Bethlehem

SIGN OF THE CROSS

Leader: In the name of the Father, and of the Son, and of the Holy Spirit.
R/. Amen.

SCRIPTURE READING

Leader: The Third Joyful Mystery, *The Birth of Jesus in the Stable at Bethlehem*. This mystery centers on the truth of the Incarnation and our response of worship before Our Lord, Who is indeed God made man. In this mystery, we reflect on Jesus being adored as King by His Mother Mary, His guardian Joseph, the shepherds and the Three Kings. In this mystery, we find the inspiration for our desire to enthrone the image of the Incarnate Redeemer, and for our constant adoration of Him.

Someone other than the leader reads:
A reading from the Holy Gospel according to Luke.

In those days a decree went out from Caesar Augustus that all the world should be enrolled. This was the first enrollment, when Quirinius was governor of Syria. And all went to be enrolled, each to his own city. And Joseph also went up from Galilee, from the city of Nazareth, to Judea, to the city of David, which is called Bethlehem, because he was of the house and lineage of David, to be enrolled with Mary his betrothed, who was with child.

And while they were there, the time came for her to be delivered. And she gave birth to her first-born son and wrapped him in swaddling cloths, and laid him in a manger, because there was no place for them in the inn. And in that region there were shepherds out in the field, keeping watch over their flock by night. And an angel of the Lord appeared to them, and the glory of the Lord shone around them, and they were filled with fear. And the angel said to them, "Be not afraid; for behold, I bring you good news of a great joy which will come to all the people; for to you is born this day in the city of David a Savior, who is Christ the Lord. And this will be a sign for you: you will find a baby wrapped in swaddling clothes and lying in a manger." And suddenly there was with the angel a multitude of the heavenly host praising God and saying, "Glory to God in the highest, and on earth peace among men with whom he is pleased."

When the angels went away from them into heaven, the shepherds said to one another, "Let us go over to Bethlehem and see this thing that has happened, which the Lord has made known to us." And they went with haste, and found Mary and Joseph, and the baby lying in a manger. And when they saw it they made known the saying which had been told them concerning this child; and all who heard it wondered at what the shepherds told them. But Mary kept all these things, pondering them in her heart. And the shepherds returned, glorifying and praising God for all they had heard and seen, as it had been told them. (Luke 2:1-20)

The Word of the Lord.
R/. Thanks be to God.

PRAYER

The Third Joyful Mystery
The Birth of Our Lord

LITANY OF THE SACRED HEART

Leader: Lord, have mercy.
R/. Christ, have mercy.

Leader: Lord, have mercy. Christ, hear us.
R/. Christ, graciously hear us.

Leader: God, the Father of Heaven,
R/. have mercy on us.

Leader: God the Son, Redeemer of the world,
R/. have mercy on us.

Leader: God the Holy Spirit,
R/. have mercy on us.

Holy Trinity, one God,
R/. have mercy on us.

Heart of Jesus, Son of the eternal Father, **R/.**
Heart of Jesus, formed by the Holy Spirit in the womb of the Virgin Mother, **R/.**
Heart of Jesus, substantially united to the Word of God, **R/.**
Heart of Jesus, of infinite majesty, **R/.**
Heart of Jesus, sacred temple of God, **R/.**
Heart of Jesus, tabernacle of the Most High, **R/.**
Heart of Jesus, house of God and gate of Heaven, **R/.**
Heart of Jesus, burning furnace of charity, **R/.**
Heart of Jesus, abode of justice and love, **R/.**
Heart of Jesus, full of goodness and love, **R/.**
Heart of Jesus, abyss of all virtues, **R/.**
Heart of Jesus, most worthy of all praise, **R/.**
Heart of Jesus, King and center of all hearts, **R/.**
Heart of Jesus, in Whom are all the treasures of wisdom and knowledge, **R/.**
Heart of Jesus, in Whom dwells the fullness of divinity, **R/.**
Heart of Jesus, in Whom the Father was well pleased, **R/.**
Heart of Jesus, of Whose fullness we have all received, **R/.**
Heart of Jesus, desire of the everlasting hills, **R/.**
Heart of Jesus, patient and most merciful, **R/.**
Heart of Jesus, enriching all who invoke Thee, **R/.**
Heart of Jesus, fountain of life and holiness, **R/.**
Heart of Jesus, propitiation for our sins, **R/.**

Heart of Jesus, loaded down with opprobrium, **R/.**
Heart of Jesus, bruised for our offenses, **R/.**
Heart of Jesus, obedient unto death, **R/.**
Heart of Jesus, pierced with a lance, **R/.**
Heart of Jesus, source of all consolation, **R/.**
Heart of Jesus, our life and resurrection, **R/.**
Heart of Jesus, our peace and reconciliation, **R/.**
Heart of Jesus, victim for sin, **R/.**
Heart of Jesus, salvation of those who trust in Thee, **R/.**
Heart of Jesus, hope of those who die in Thee, **R/.**
Heart of Jesus, delight of all the saints, **R/.**

Leader: Lamb of God, Who takes away the sins of the world,
R/. spare us, O Lord.

Leader: Lamb of God, Who takes away the sins of the world,
R/. graciously hear us, O Lord.

Leader: Lamb of God, Who takes away the sins of the world,
R/. have mercy on us.

Leader: Jesus, meek and humble of Heart,
R/. make our hearts like unto Thine.

PRAYER

Leader: Let us pray. Sacred Heart of Jesus, we salute You, for You are the King of Kings, the Ruler of families and nations. But, sad to say, in many nations You have been dethroned and Your rights rejected. This is mainly because You were first dethroned in many families of which nations are composed.

Loving Master, we want to make up for this insult to Your Divine Majesty by lovingly enthroning You as King of our family. Like Mary and Joseph, like the shepherds and the Three Kings, we want to give You a royal welcome as they did when they adored You in Your humble home at Bethlehem.

Like them, we have no royal throne to offer You, but we can and we will offer something even more pleasing to You. In our home, Your throne will be a living throne, the loyal hearts of the members of this family; Your royal crown, our acts of love. O Mary, Queen of our home, by your loving submission to the will of God in all things, obtain for us the grace never to sadden the Heart of our King by willful disobedience to His Commandments or to those of His Church. May it be said of each of us what the Gospel says of Jesus, "He was obedient to them."

Good Saint Joseph, guardian of our family, help us to make our Enthronement the beginning of a new life of love in our home. Through the presence of the Sacred Heart of Jesus in our family circle, and through your powerful intercession, may we receive the grace to know our King more personally, love Him more ardently, and thus serve Him more faithfully. Amen.

INDULGENCED PRAYER

All: O Christ Jesus, I acknowledge You to be King of the universe; all that has been made is created by You. Exercise over me all Your sovereign rights. I hereby renew the promises of my Baptism, renouncing Satan and all his pomps and works, and I engage myself to lead henceforth a truly Christian life. And in a special manner do I undertake to bring about the triumph of the rights of God and His Church, so far as in me lies. Divine Heart of Jesus, I offer You my poor actions to obtain the acknowledgment by every heart of Your sacred kingly power. In such wisdom may the kingdom of Your peace be firmly established throughout all the earth.

Leader: Most Sacred Heart of Jesus,
R/. Thy Kingdom come through Mary.

Leader: Sacred Heart of Jesus,
R/. protect our families.

Leader: Immaculate Heart of Mary, Queen of Heaven and of our home,
R/. pray for us.

Leader: Saint Joseph, friend of the Sacred Heart,
R/. pray for us.

Leader: Saint Michael, first champion of the Kingship of Christ,
R/. pray for us.

Leader: Guardian Angels of our family,
R/. pray for us.

HYMN

Immaculate Mary
Melody is on page 175.

1. Immaculate Mary, thy praises we sing,
   Who reignest in splendor with Jesus our King.
   Ave, Ave, Ave María! Ave, Ave María!

2. In heaven the blessed thy glory proclaim,
   On earth we thy children invoke thy fair name.
   Ave, Ave, Ave María! Ave, Ave María!

3. Thy name is our power, thy virtues our light,
   Thy love is our comfort, thy pleading our might.
   Ave, Ave, Ave, María! Ave, Ave, María!

4. We pray for our Mother, the Church upon earth,
   And bless, sweetest Lady, the land of our birth.
   Ave, Ave, Ave Maria! Ave, Ave Maria!

THE SECOND DAY

To the Heart of Our Brother, Jesus of Nazareth

SIGN OF THE CROSS

Leader: In the name of the Father, and of the Son, and of the Holy Spirit.

R/. Amen.

SCRIPTURE READING

Leader: The Fifth Joyful Mystery, *The Finding of the Child Jesus in the Temple, and His Return to Nazareth.* This mystery inspires us to model the life of our family upon the Holy Family as we think of Jesus, the Son of God, living an ordinary life in the little home at Nazareth with Mary and Joseph. The care of Mary and Joseph for Jesus and His obedience to them are models for our relationships within the family as well as with others.

Someone other than the leader reads:
A reading from the Holy Gospel according to Luke.

And the child grew and became strong, filled with wisdom; and the favor of God was upon him. Now his parents went to Jerusalem every year at the feast of the Passover. And when he was twelve years old, they went up according to custom; and when the feast was ended, as they were returning, the boy Jesus stayed behind in Jerusalem. His parents did not know it, but supposing him to be in the company they went a day's journey, and they sought him among their kinsfolk and acquaintances; and when they did not find him, they returned to Jerusalem, seeking him.

After three days they found him in the temple, sitting among the teachers, listening to them and asking them questions; and all who heard him were amazed at his understanding and his answers. And when they saw him they were astonished; and his mother said to him, "Son, why have you treated us so? Behold, your father and I have been looking for you anxiously." And he said to them, "How is it that you sought me? Did you not know that I must be in my Father's house?" And they did not understand the saying which he spoke to them. And he went down with them and came to Nazareth, and was obedient to them; and his mother kept all these things in her heart. And Jesus increased in wisdom and in stature, and in favor with God and man. (Luke 2:40-52)

The Word of the Lord.
R/. Thanks be to God.

PRAYER

The Fifth Joyful Mystery
The Finding of the Child Jesus in the Temple

LITANY OF THE SACRED HEART

Leader: Lord, have mercy.
R/. Christ, have mercy.

Leader: Lord, have mercy. Christ, hear us.
R/. Christ, graciously hear us.

Leader: God, the Father of Heaven,
R/. have mercy on us.

Leader: God the Son, Redeemer of the world,
R/. have mercy on us.

Leader: God the Holy Spirit,
R/. have mercy on us.

Holy Trinity, one God,
R/. have mercy on us.

Heart of Jesus, Son of the eternal Father, **R/.**
Heart of Jesus, formed by the Holy Spirit in the womb of the Virgin Mother, **R/.**
Heart of Jesus, substantially united to the Word of God, **R/.**
Heart of Jesus, of infinite majesty, **R/.**
Heart of Jesus, sacred temple of God, **R/.**
Heart of Jesus, tabernacle of the Most High, **R/.**
Heart of Jesus, house of God and gate of Heaven, **R/.**
Heart of Jesus, burning furnace of charity, **R/.**
Heart of Jesus, abode of justice and love, **R/.**
Heart of Jesus, full of goodness and love, **R/.**
Heart of Jesus, abyss of all virtues, **R/.**
Heart of Jesus, most worthy of all praise, **R/.**
Heart of Jesus, King and center of all hearts, **R/.**
Heart of Jesus, in Whom are all the treasures of wisdom and knowledge, **R/.**
Heart of Jesus, in Whom dwells the fullness of divinity, **R/.**
Heart of Jesus, in Whom the Father was well pleased, **R/.**
Heart of Jesus, of Whose fullness we have all received, **R/.**

Heart of Jesus, desire of the everlasting hills, **R/.**
Heart of Jesus, patient and most merciful, **R/.**
Heart of Jesus, enriching all who invoke Thee, **R/.**
Heart of Jesus, fountain of life and holiness, **R/.**
Heart of Jesus, propitiation for our sins, **R/.**
Heart of Jesus, loaded down with opprobrium, **R/.**
Heart of Jesus, bruised for our offenses, **R/.**
Heart of Jesus, obedient unto death, **R/.**
Heart of Jesus, pierced with a lance, **R/.**
Heart of Jesus, source of all consolation, **R/.**
Heart of Jesus, our life and resurrection, **R/.**
Heart of Jesus, our peace and reconciliation, **R/.**
Heart of Jesus, victim for sin, **R/.**
Heart of Jesus, salvation of those who trust in Thee, **R/.**
Heart of Jesus, hope of those who die in Thee, **R/.**
Heart of Jesus, delight of all the saints, **R/.**

Leader: Lamb of God, Who takes away the sins of the world,
R/. spare us, O Lord.

Leader: Lamb of God, Who takes away the sins of the world,
R/. graciously hear us, O Lord.

Leader: Lamb of God, Who takes away the sins of the world,
R/. have mercy on us.

Leader: Jesus, meek and humble of Heart,
R/. make our hearts like unto Thine.

PRAYER

Leader: Let us pray. Dear Jesus, Son of God, when we call You "Brother," we speak the truth, for You are indeed just that. Saint John told us so when in his Gospel he wrote: "But to as many as received Him, He gave the power of becoming sons of God." Therefore we are Your adopted brothers and sisters and co-heirs of Heaven. But since You are a King, we too, have the privilege of being members of a royal family, as were Mary and Joseph.

How honored will we be to have our Brother-King come to dwell in our humble home in order to share our joys and sorrows! Once You are enthroned in our family, we will understand as never before the meaning of these words, "And the Word was made flesh and dwelt among us." No longer need we envy Mary and Joseph at Nazareth, for Your abiding presence in our home will make our family another Nazareth wherein we will vie with one another in giving You proofs of our love. We will do this especially by the practice of family charity, trying to love each other as You have loved us.

O Mary, Queen of Nazareth, Mother of Jesus, obtain for us the grace to appreciate the presence of your Divine Son enthroned in our home. Grant us a greater love for Jesus ever present in the Blessed Sacrament, a deeper love for Holy Mass, a more ardent longing to unite ourselves as often as possible with our loving Savior in Holy Communion.

Good Saint Joseph, you were privileged to share the joys and sorrows of your foster-Son at Nazareth. Teach us how to share our everyday joys and sorrows with our Brother Jesus, here on earth, so that one day our entire family may join Mary and you in sharing the joys of Heaven, where we will see our King and Brother face to face and, with you, love, adore, thank and praise Him for all eternity. Amen.

INDULGENCED PRAYER

All: O Christ Jesus, I acknowledge You to be King of the universe; all that has been made is created by You. Exercise over me all Your sovereign rights. I hereby renew the promises of my Baptism, renouncing Satan and all his pomps and works, and I engage myself to lead henceforth a truly Christian life. And in a special manner do I undertake to bring about the triumph of the rights of God and His Church, so far as in me lies. Divine Heart of Jesus, I offer You my poor actions to obtain the acknowledgment by every heart of Your sacred kingly power. In such wisdom may the kingdom of Your peace be firmly established throughout all the earth.

Leader: Eucharistic Heart of Jesus,
R/. Thy Kingdom come in our home.

Leader: Our Lady of the Blessed Sacrament,
R/. pray for us.

Leader: Saint Joseph, foster-father of Our Lord Jesus Christ and true spouse of Mary the Virgin,
R/. pray for us.

Leader: Saints Joachim and Anne, parents of the Blessed Virgin Mary,
R/. pray for us.

Leader: Guardian Angels of our family,
R/. pray for us.

HYMN

To Jesus Christ, Our Sov'reign King

Melody is on page 172.

1. To Jesus Christ, our Sov'reign King,
   Who is the world's salvation,
   All praise and homage do we bring,
   And thanks and adoration.

Refrain: Christ Jesus Victor...

2. Thy reign extend, O King benign,
   To ev'ry land and nation,
   For in Thy kingdom, Lord divine,
   Alone we find salvation.

Refrain: Christ Jesus Victor...

3. To Thee and to Thy Church, great King,
   We pledge our hearts' oblation,
   Until before Thy throne we sing,
   In endless jubilation.

Refrain: Christ Jesus Victor...

4. Thy majesty shall be the praise
   And thanks of ev'ry nation,
   To thee the world with joy shall raise
   The voice of exultation.

Refrain: Christ Jesus Victor...

5. May God the Father, God the Son,
   And God the Spirit bless us!
   Let all the world praise him alone,
   Let solemn awe possess us.

Refrain: Christ Jesus Victor...

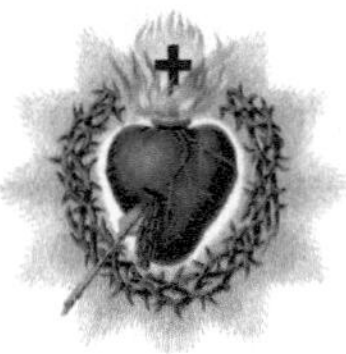

THE THIRD DAY

To the Heart of Our Friend, Jesus of Bethany

SIGN OF THE CROSS

Leader: In the name of the Father, and of the Son, and of the Holy Spirit.
R/. Amen.

SCRIPTURE READING

Leader: The First Glorious Mystery, *The Resurrection.* Reflecting on this mystery helps us to recognize the living presence of Our Lord with us in the Church, and increases in us the desire to be with Him always. We think of Jesus rising in triumph from the tomb and hear Him promising Martha and Mary that their brother will rise again.

Someone other than the leader reads:

A reading from the Holy Gospel according to Luke.

Now a certain man was ill, Lazarus of Bethany, the village of Mary and her sister Martha. It was Mary who anointed the Lord with ointment and wiped his feet with her hair, whose brother Lazarus was ill. So the sisters sent to him, saying, "Lord, he whom you love is ill."

But when Jesus heard it he said, "This illness is not unto death; it is for the glory of God, so that the Son of God may be glorified by means of it." Now Jesus loved Martha and her sister and Lazarus. So when he heard that he was ill, he stayed two days longer in the place where he was. Then after this he said to the disciples, "Let us go into Judea again." The disciples said to him, "Rabbi, the Jews were but now seeking to stone you, and are you going there again?" Jesus answered, "Are there not twelve hours in the day? If any one walks in the day, he does not stumble, because he sees the light of this world. But if any one walks in the night, he stumbles, because the light is not in him." Thus he spoke, and then he said to them, "Our friend Lazarus has fallen asleep, but I go to awake him out of sleep." The disciples said to him, "Lord, if he has fallen asleep, he will recover." Now Jesus had spoken of his death, but they thought that he meant taking rest in sleep. Then Jesus told them plainly, "Lazarus is dead; and for your sake I am glad that I was not there, so that you may believe. But let us go to him." Thomas, called the Twin, said to his fellow disciples, "Let us also go, that we may die with him."

Now when Jesus came, he found that Lazarus had already been in the tomb four days. Bethany was near Jerusalem, about two miles off, and many of the Jews had come to Martha and Mary to console them concerning their brother. When Martha heard that Jesus was coming, she went and met him, while Mary sat in the house. Martha said to Jesus, "Lord, if you had been here, my brother would not have died. And even now I know that whatever you ask from God, God will give you." Jesus said to her, "Your brother will rise again." Martha said to him, "I know that he will rise again in the resurrection at the last day." Jesus said to her, "I am the resurrection and the life; he who believes in me, though he die, yet shall he live, and whoever lives and believes in me shall never die. Do you believe this?" She said to him, "Yes, Lord; I believe that you are the Christ, the Son of God, he who is coming into the world." (John 11:1-27)

The Word of the Lord.
R/. Thanks be to God.

PRAYER

The First Glorious Mystery
The Resurrection of Jesus

LITANY OF THE SACRED HEART

Leader: Lord, have mercy.
R/. Christ, have mercy.

Leader: Lord, have mercy. Christ, hear us.
R/. Christ, graciously hear us.

Leader: God, the Father of Heaven,
R/. have mercy on us.

Leader: God the Son, Redeemer of the world,
R/. have mercy on us.

Leader: God the Holy Spirit,
R/. have mercy on us.

Holy Trinity, one God,
R/. have mercy on us.

Heart of Jesus, Son of the eternal Father, **R/.**
Heart of Jesus, formed by the Holy Spirit in the womb of the Virgin Mother, **R/.**
Heart of Jesus, substantially united to the Word of God, **R/.**
Heart of Jesus, of infinite majesty, **R/.**
Heart of Jesus, sacred temple of God, **R/.**
Heart of Jesus, tabernacle of the Most High, **R/.**
Heart of Jesus, house of God and gate of Heaven, **R/.**
Heart of Jesus, burning furnace of charity, **R/.**
Heart of Jesus, abode of justice and love, **R/.**
Heart of Jesus, full of goodness and love, **R/.**
Heart of Jesus, abyss of all virtues, **R/.**
Heart of Jesus, most worthy of all praise, **R/.**
Heart of Jesus, King and center of all hearts, **R/.**
Heart of Jesus, in Whom are all the treasures of wisdom and knowledge, **R/.**
Heart of Jesus, in Whom dwells the fullness of divinity, **R/.**

Heart of Jesus, in Whom the Father was well pleased, **R/.**
Heart of Jesus, of Whose fullness we have all received, **R/.**
Heart of Jesus, desire of the everlasting hills, **R/.**
Heart of Jesus, patient and most merciful, **R/.**
Heart of Jesus, enriching all who invoke Thee, **R/.**
Heart of Jesus, fountain of life and holiness, **R/.**
Heart of Jesus, propitiation for our sins, **R/.**
Heart of Jesus, loaded down with opprobrium, **R/.**
Heart of Jesus, bruised for our offenses, **R/.**
Heart of Jesus, obedient unto death, **R/.**
Heart of Jesus, pierced with a lance, **R/.**
Heart of Jesus, source of all consolation, **R/.**
Heart of Jesus, our life and resurrection, **R/.**
Heart of Jesus, our peace and reconciliation, **R/.**
Heart of Jesus, victim for sin, **R/.**
Heart of Jesus, salvation of those who trust in Thee, **R/.**
Heart of Jesus, hope of those who die in Thee, **R/.**
Heart of Jesus, delight of all the saints, **R/.**

Leader: Lamb of God, Who takes away the sins of the world,
R/. spare us, O Lord.

Leader: Lamb of God, Who takes away the sins of the world,
R/. graciously hear us, O Lord.

Leader: Lamb of God, Who takes away the sins of the world,
R/. have mercy on us.

Leader: Jesus, meek and humble of Heart,
R/. make our hearts like unto Thine.

PRAYER

Leader: Let us pray. "My delights are to be with the children of men." These words from the *Book of Proverbs* were certainly spoken about You, dear Jesus, Who came down to share our exile here below. You delight in being with us because we need You and You are our best Friend. You love all without exception: saints and sinners, the rich and the poor, the learned and the uneducated. You love all races and all peoples, but, above all, you love all families. You proved that love by spending thirty years in Your home at Nazareth, and during Your public life, many times You accepted invitations to visit families. You even told Zacchaeus the sinner, "I must stay in thy house today."

But there was one family for whom You had a special love, that of Lazarus, Martha and Mary. How many times did You not stay with that beloved family at Bethany! It was there You found rest and solace after the fatigue of Your labors and the insulting attacks of Your enemies. At Bethany, You were always received as a royal Guest, but also You were treated as a Brother and a Friend.

Dear Jesus, once You are enthroned in our home, we, too, want to be Your true friends. We want You to feel at home with us. We will try to console You for those who do not love You. We will serve You like Martha, listen to You like Mary, and thank You as did Lazarus. We feel confident that You will richly bless our family as You did the family of Lazarus and all those families who invited You into their homes.

And if there are in our homes prodigal sons, lost sheep, sinners dead to the life of grace, we know that You will say to them as You did to Zacchaeus, "Today salvation has come to this house." You will be to them a loving Father, a Good

Shepherd, a Divine Physician, for You are "the Resurrection and the Life."

O Mary, Mother of our best Friend, and Saint Joseph, our patron, obtain for us the grace to make our home a true Bethany of the Sacred Heart. May our friendship with Jesus be loving, loyal and lasting. May our daily living with our King and our Guest bring about a closer union of hearts, minds and wills so that our entire family, united with the Heart of Jesus here on earth, may remain united with Him and the Father and the Holy Spirit in our true home, Heaven, for all eternity! Amen.

INDULGENCED PRAYER

All: O Christ Jesus, I acknowledge You to be King of the universe; all that has been made is created by You. Exercise over me all Your sovereign rights. I hereby renew the promises of my Baptism, renouncing Satan and all his pomps and works, and I engage myself to lead henceforth a truly Christian life. And in a special manner do I undertake to bring about the triumph of the rights of God and His Church, so far as in me lies. Divine Heart of Jesus, I offer You my poor actions to obtain the acknowledgment by every heart of Your sacred kingly power. In such wisdom may the kingdom of Your peace be firmly established throughout all the earth.

Leader: Heart of Jesus, King, Brother and Friend of our family, we welcome You to our home.
R/. Thy Kingdom come.

Leader: Our Lady of the Sacred Heart,
R/. pray for us.

Leader: Saint Joseph, model and patron of lovers of the Sacred Heart,
R/. pray for us.

Leader: Saints Lazarus, Martha, and Mary,
R/. pray for us.

Leader: Guardian Angels of our family,
R/. pray for us.

Leader: O Jesus, Friend of little children,
R/. bless the little children of the whole world.

HYMN

Holy God, We Praise Thy Name

Melody is on page 174.

1. Holy God, we praise thy name!
   Lord of all, we bow before thee!
   All on Earth thy sceptre claim,
   All in Heav'n above adore thee;
   Infinite thy vast domain,
   Everlasting is thy reign.

2. Hark! the loud celestial hymn
   Angel choirs above are raising!
   Cherubim and seraphim,
   In unceasing chorus praising,
   Fill the heav'ns with sweet accord;
   Holy, holy, holy, Lord!

3. Lo! The blessed Twelve proclaim
   To the Father hymns of glory;
   Prophets sing in loud acclaim;
   Martyrs tell the wondrous story;
   And from morn to set of sun
   Through the Church they sing as one.

4. Holy Father, Holy Son,
   Holy Spirit, Three we name thee,
   While in essence only One,
   Undivided God we claim thee;
   And adoring bend the knee,
   While we own the mystery.

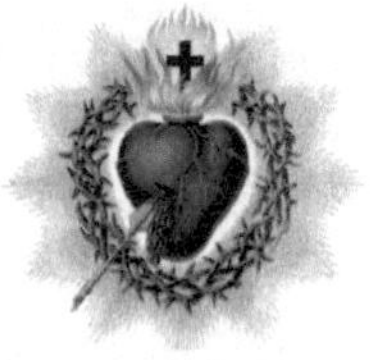

CEREMONY *for the* ENTHRONEMENT *of the* SACRED HEART IN THE HOME

After all the arrangements have been made, the Enthronement Ceremony begins at a table on which the image of the Sacred Heart and holy water have been placed. This table should be somewhat distant from the place of Enthronement in order to form a procession to the place of Enthronement. The priest will bless the image during the Enthronement Ceremony, but if a priest is not present, the image should be blessed beforehand, and the head of the house assumes the role of leader.

OPENING HYMN

Melody is on page 172.

To Jesus Christ, Our Sov'reign King

1. To Jesus Christ, our Sov'reign King,
   Who is the world's salvation,
   All praise and homage do we bring,
   And thanks and adoration.

Refrain: Christ Jesus Victor...

2. Thy reign extend, O King benign,
   To ev'ry land and nation,
   For in Thy kingdom, Lord divine,
   Alone we find salvation.

Refrain: Christ Jesus Victor...

3. To Thee and to Thy Church, great King,
   We pledge our hearts' oblation,
   Until before Thy throne we sing,
   In endless jubilation.

Refrain: Christ Jesus Victor...

4. Thy majesty shall be the praise
   And thanks of ev'ry nation,
   To thee the world with joy shall raise
   The voice of exultation.

Refrain: Christ Jesus Victor...

5. May God the Father, God the Son,
   And God the Spirit bless us!
   Let all the world praise him alone,
   Let solemn awe possess us.

Refrain: Christ Jesus Victor...

SIGN OF THE CROSS

Leader: In the name of the Father, and of the Son, and of the Holy Spirit.
R/. Amen.

INTRODUCTION

Leader: "God is Love" (1 John 4:16), and all of His works serve to show this divine love to mankind. The writings of the Old Testament reveal that God's love created us in His image and likeness; it established a covenant with Abraham; it rescued the Chosen People from slavery in Egypt and brought them to the Promised Land. The fullest expression of God's love is the Person of Jesus Christ: "For God so loved the world that He gave His only-begotten Son, that whoever believes in Him should not perish but have eternal life" (John 3:16). The Heart of Jesus Itself, in love with and wounded for mankind, is the most perfect symbol of the love of God. For this reason, "The prayer of the Church venerates and honors the Heart of Jesus.... It adores the Incarnate Word and His Heart which, out of love for men, He allowed to be pierced by our sins" (*Catechism of the Catholic Church*, n. 2669).

The Enthronement of the Sacred Heart of Jesus, for which we are gathered, is an expression of our own love of God and the love which He shows to us. The enthroned image of the Sacred Heart expresses the true Kingship of Christ Who rules over us by giving up His life for us. It daily reminds each member of the family to follow in Christ's royal way by making reparation for sins and striving to serve God and neighbor more lovingly.

The image of the Sacred Heart of Jesus is enthroned to signify that Christ is He Who gives inspiration and direction to each member of the family. The Enthronement is a single act, but it represents a way of life by which each member of the family is transformed in Christ each day.

May the Enthronement truly be for this family a source of new vigor in living the Christian vocation, the vocation to love.

APOSTLES' CREED

Leader: As an act of loving faith in all of Jesus' teachings, and as an act of atonement for those who reject them or do not practice them, let us recite the Apostles' Creed together.

All: I believe in God, the Father Almighty,
Creator of Heaven and earth;
and in Jesus Christ, His only Son, Our Lord;
Who was conceived by the Holy Spirit,
born of the Virgin Mary,
suffered under Pontius Pilate, was crucified, died, and was buried.
He descended into Hell;
the third day He arose again from the dead.
He ascended into Heaven, and sits at the right hand of God, the Father Almighty;
from thence He shall come to judge the living and the dead.

I believe in the Holy Spirit,
the Holy Catholic Church,
the Communion of Saints, the forgiveness of sins,
the resurrection of the body and life everlasting.
Amen.

SCRIPTURE READING

Someone other than the leader reads:
A reading from the First Letter of John.

Beloved, let us love one another; for love is of God, and he who loves is born of God and knows God. He who does not love does not know God; for God is love. In this the love of God was made manifest among us, that God sent his only-begotten Son into the world, so that we might live through him. In this is love, not that we loved God but that he loved us and sent his Son to be the expiation for our sins.

Beloved, if God so loved us, we also ought to love one another. No man has ever seen God; if we love one another, God abides in us and his love is perfected in us. By this we know that we abide in him and he in us, because he has given us of his own Spirit. And we have seen and testify that the Father has sent his Son as the Savior of the world. Whoever confesses that Jesus is the Son of God, God abides in him, and he in God. So we know and believe the love God has for us. (1 John 4:7-16a)

The Word of the Lord.
R/. Thanks be to God.

Other readings may be used, particularly the account of the Annunciation (Luke 1:26-33), Our Lord's meeting with Zacchaeus (Luke 19:1-10) or Our Lord's visit to the home of Martha and Mary (Luke 10:38-41).

REFLECTION (optional)

A brief reflection may be offered by the leader.

BLESSING OF THE IMAGE

The image of the Sacred Heart is to be blessed by a priest. If an image of the Immaculate Heart of Mary is installed along with the Sacred Heart, the blessing found on page 143 may be used. If the images were previously blessed, the blessings are omitted at this time.

Priest:
Lord,
although Your glory lies beyond our sight,
out of Your great love
You have revealed Yourself in the Heart of Christ.
Bless [*sprinkle holy water*] this image of Your Son.
May those who venerate it
honor Christ by growing in His likeness,
Who is Lord for ever and ever.

R/. Amen.

The priest sprinkles the image with holy water.

ACT OF ENTHRONEMENT

For the procession, the head of the household carries the image of the Sacred Heart, another family member carries the Bible, and others may carry candles. The head of the household, accompanied by the priest or deacon, members of the household, and guests then processes with the image to the place of Enthronement. The head of the household enthrones the image of the Sacred Heart in the selected place saying:

I now enthrone Jesus as King and Friend of our family.

The person carrying the Bible then places it near the image of the Sacred Heart and says:

We are nourished by the Body and Blood of Christ, and by the Word of God.

The candles are then placed on either side of the image as the candle bearers (or all present, if there are no candle bearers) say the following together:

The Lord sits enthroned as King forever! (Psalm 29:10b)
All that the Lord has spoken we will do, and we will be obedient. (Exodus 24:7)

ACT OF CONSECRATION OF THE FAMILY

All kneel and say in unison:

O Sacred Heart of Jesus, Who made known to Saint Margaret Mary Your great desire to reign over Christian families, we are gathered here today to proclaim Your complete rule over our family. From now on we promise to lead a Christ-like life: we will strive to develop in our home all the virtues which bring with them the peace that You promised. And we will not compromise with the spirit of secularism which You have so strongly denounced.

You will rule over our minds through our deep and living faith. You will be King of our hearts by our generous love for You; and we will cultivate this love by the frequent reception of You in Holy Communion.

Divine Heart of Jesus, preside over our family gatherings; bless all our family undertakings, both spiritual and temporal. Sanctify our joys and comfort us in our sorrows. And if any member of our family should have the misfortune to offend You seriously, remind him, O Sacred Heart of Jesus, of Your infinite love and mercy for the penitent sinner.

And when the hour of separation comes, when death brings its sorrows into our family, whether we go or whether we stay, we will humbly accept Your Divine Will. And at the same time we will console and comfort ourselves with the thought that the time will come when our whole family will be united lovingly with You in Heaven forever. There we shall sing a hymn of praise to the infinite mercy and love of Your Sacred Heart.

We ask the Immaculate Heart of Mary and our glorious protector, Saint Joseph, to offer You this family Consecration.

May the memory of this consecration be with us always. Glory to the Divine Heart of Jesus, our King!

Praise to the Divine Heart of Jesus that brought us salvation. To It be honor and glory forever.

Amen.

If an image of the Immaculate Heart of Mary is installed, the Act of Consecration to the Immaculate Heart found on page 143 is made at this point.

INTERCESSIONS

Leader: Lord Jesus, You told us that "whatever you ask the Father in my name, he will give to you." In Your name, and with great confidence in Your love, we now offer these prayers:

Someone other than the leader proposes the intercessions:

For the grace of being faithful to this covenant with Jesus and our renewed way of life in Him, let us pray:
R/. Lord, hear our prayer.

For an increase of personal, generous love for Jesus, and a greater trust in His merciful love, let us pray:
R/. Lord, hear our prayer.

That the Holy Spirit may always find our hearts responsive to His call, let us pray:
R/. Lord, hear our prayer.

For a deeper appreciation of the greatest gift of the Heart of Jesus, the Holy Eucharist, through frequent participation in the Holy Sacrifice of the Mass and Holy Communion, especially on First Fridays, let us pray:
R/. Lord, hear our prayer.

That we may desire to receive the Sacrament of Confession more often in order to increase our love for Jesus and to avoid sin, let us pray:
R/. Lord, hear our prayer.

That our family members who are absent may be protected in all they do, and that all our beloved family who have died may be united to the Heart of Jesus in Heaven for ever, let us pray:
R/. Lord, hear our prayer.

Leader:
God our Father,
through the Sacred Heart of Your Son, Jesus,
You pour forth Your eternal love upon us.
By the enthronement of the image of Jesus' Heart
and our consecration to It,
may we show our love to You and to the world.
We ask this through the same Christ Our Lord.

R/. Amen.

Leader: Let us conclude by calling on the Mother of God, Mary Most Holy:

HAIL HOLY QUEEN

All: Hail, Holy Queen, Mother of Mercy, our life, our sweetness, and our hope! To thee do we cry, poor banished children of Eve; to thee do we send up our sighs, mourning and weeping in this valley of tears. Turn then, most gracious advocate, thine eyes of mercy toward us, and after this our exile, show unto us the blessed fruit of thy womb, Jesus. O clement, O loving, O sweet Virgin Mary.

Leader: Pray for us, O holy Mother of God.
R/. That we may be made worthy of the promises of Christ.
Leader: Most Sacred Heart of Jesus,
R/. have mercy on us.

Leader: Immaculate Heart of Mary,
R/. pray for us!

Leader: Saint Joseph,
R/. pray for us!

Leader: Our Guardian Angels,
R/. pray for us!

Leader: Most Sacred Heart of Jesus,
R/. have mercy on us.

CLOSING PRAYER

Leader: Let us pray. O Father of mercies and God of all consolation, Who by the exceeding love with which You have loved us, have given us the Heart of Your beloved Son so that having but one heart with Him, we may love You perfectly, grant, we beseech You, that our hearts, being consumed in unity with the Heart of Jesus and with one another, may perform all our works in accord with His humility and charity and that, by His mediation, the just desires of our hearts may be accomplished, through the same Christ Our Lord.

R/. Amen.

If a priest is present, the Rite of Enthronement concludes with a blessing. Otherwise, the Rite concludes with the ***Sign of the Cross****.*

BLESSING AND DISMISSAL

Priest: The Lord be with you.
R/. And with your spirit.

Priest: May almighty God bless you, the Father, the Son, and [*sprinkle holy water*] the Holy Spirit.
R/. Amen.

Priest: Go in peace.
R/. Thanks be to God.

CLOSING HYMN

Holy God, We Praise Thy Name

Melody is on page 174.

1. Holy God, we praise thy name!
   Lord of all, we bow before thee!
   All on Earth thy sceptre claim,
   All in Heav'n above adore thee;
   Infinite thy vast domain,
   Everlasting is thy reign.

2. Hark! the loud celestial hymn
   Angel choirs above are raising!
   Cherubim and seraphim,
   In unceasing chorus praising,
   Fill the heav'ns with sweet accord;
   Holy, holy, holy, Lord!

3. Lo! The blessed Twelve proclaim
   To the Father hymns of glory;
   Prophets sing in loud acclaim;
   Martyrs tell the wondrous story;
   And from morn to set of sun
   Through the Church they sing as one.

4. Holy Father, Holy Son,
   Holy Spirit, Three we name thee,
   While in essence only One,
   Undivided God we claim thee;
   And adoring bend the knee,
   While we own the mystery.

*The **Certificate of Enthronement** found on page 179 may be downloaded and signed at this time.*

TRIDUUM *of* PRAYERS *for the* ENTHRONEMENT IN PARISHES, CATHOLIC SCHOOLS, AND OTHER SETTINGS

THE FIRST DAY

To the Heart of Our King, Jesus of Bethlehem

SIGN OF THE CROSS

Leader: In the name of the Father, and of the Son, and of the Holy Spirit.
R/. Amen.

SCRIPTURE READING

Leader: The Third Joyful Mystery, *The Birth of Jesus in the Stable at Bethlehem*. This mystery centers on the truth of the Incarnation and our response of worship before Our Lord, Who is indeed God made man. In this mystery, we reflect on Jesus being adored as King by His Mother Mary, His guardian Joseph, the shepherds and the Three Kings. In this mystery, we find the inspiration for our desire to enthrone the image of the Incarnate Redeemer, and for our constant adoration of Him.

Someone other than the leader reads:

A reading from the Holy Gospel according to Luke.

In those days a decree went out from Caesar Augustus that all the world should be enrolled. This was the first enrollment, when Quirinius was governor of Syria. And all went to be enrolled, each to his own city. And Joseph also went up from Galilee, from the city of Nazareth, to Judea, to the city of David, which is called Bethlehem, because he was of the house and lineage of David, to be enrolled with Mary his betrothed, who was with child.

And while they were there, the time came for her to be delivered. And she gave birth to her first-born son and wrapped him in swaddling cloths, and laid him in a manger, because there was no place for them in the inn. And in that region there were shepherds out in the field, keeping watch over their flock by night. And an angel of the Lord appeared to them, and the glory of the Lord shone around them, and they were filled with fear. And the angel said to them, "Be not afraid; for behold, I bring you good news of a great joy which will come to all the people; for to you is born this day in the city of David a Savior, who is Christ the Lord. And this will be a sign for you: you will find a baby wrapped in swaddling clothes and lying in a manger." And suddenly there was with the angel a multitude of the heavenly host praising God and saying, "Glory to God in the highest, and on earth peace among men with whom he is pleased."

When the angels went away from them into heaven, the shepherds said to one another, "Let us go over to Bethlehem and see this thing that has happened, which the Lord has made known to us." And they went with haste, and found Mary and Joseph, and the baby lying in a manger. And when they saw it they made known the saying which had been told them concerning this child; and all who heard it wondered at what the shepherds told them. But Mary kept all these things, pondering them in her heart. And the shepherds returned, glorifying and praising God for all they had heard and seen, as it had been told them. (Luke 2:1-20)

The Word of the Lord.

R/. Thanks be to God.

PRAYER

The Third Joyful Mystery
The Birth of Our Lord

LITANY OF THE SACRED HEART

Leader: Lord, have mercy.
R/. Christ, have mercy.

Leader: Lord, have mercy. Christ, hear us.
R/. Christ, graciously hear us.

Leader: God, the Father of Heaven,
R/. have mercy on us.

Leader: God the Son, Redeemer of the world,
R/. have mercy on us.

Leader: God the Holy Spirit,
R/. have mercy on us.

Holy Trinity, one God,
R/. have mercy on us.

Heart of Jesus, Son of the eternal Father, **R/.**
Heart of Jesus, formed by the Holy Spirit in the womb of the Virgin Mother, **R/.**
Heart of Jesus, substantially united to the Word of God, **R/.**
Heart of Jesus, of infinite majesty, **R/.**
Heart of Jesus, sacred temple of God, **R/.**
Heart of Jesus, tabernacle of the Most High, **R/.**
Heart of Jesus, house of God and gate of Heaven, **R/.**
Heart of Jesus, burning furnace of charity, **R/.**
Heart of Jesus, abode of justice and love, **R/.**
Heart of Jesus, full of goodness and love, **R/.**
Heart of Jesus, abyss of all virtues, **R/.**
Heart of Jesus, most worthy of all praise, **R/.**
Heart of Jesus, King and center of all hearts, **R/.**
Heart of Jesus, in Whom are all the treasures of wisdom and knowledge, **R/.**
Heart of Jesus, in Whom dwells the fullness of divinity, **R/.**

Heart of Jesus, in Whom the Father was well pleased, **R/.**
Heart of Jesus, of Whose fullness we have all received, **R/.**
Heart of Jesus, desire of the everlasting hills, **R/.**
Heart of Jesus, patient and most merciful, **R/.**
Heart of Jesus, enriching all who invoke Thee, **R/.**
Heart of Jesus, fountain of life and holiness, **R/.**
Heart of Jesus, propitiation for our sins, **R/.**
Heart of Jesus, loaded down with opprobrium, **R/.**
Heart of Jesus, bruised for our offenses, **R/.**
Heart of Jesus, obedient unto death, **R/.**
Heart of Jesus, pierced with a lance, **R/.**
Heart of Jesus, source of all consolation, **R/.**
Heart of Jesus, our life and resurrection, **R/.**
Heart of Jesus, our peace and reconciliation, **R/.**
Heart of Jesus, victim for sin, **R/.**
Heart of Jesus, salvation of those who trust in Thee, **R/.**
Heart of Jesus, hope of those who die in Thee, **R/.**
Heart of Jesus, delight of all the saints, **R/.**

Leader: Lamb of God, Who takes away the sins of the world,
R/. spare us, O Lord.

Leader: Lamb of God, Who takes away the sins of the world,
R/. graciously hear us, O Lord.

Leader: Lamb of God, Who takes away the sins of the world,
R/. have mercy on us.

Leader: Jesus, meek and humble of Heart,
R/. make our hearts like unto Thine.

PRAYER

Leader: Let us pray. Sacred Heart of Jesus, we salute You, for You are the King of Kings, the Ruler of families and nations. But, sad to say, in many nations You have been dethroned and Your rights rejected. This is mainly because You were first dethroned in many families of which nations are composed.

Loving Master, we want to make up for this insult to Your Divine Majesty by lovingly enthroning You as our King. Like Mary and Joseph, like the shepherds and the Three Kings, we want to give You a royal welcome as they did when they adored You in Your humble home at Bethlehem.

Like them, we have no royal throne to offer You, but we can and we will offer something even more pleasing to You. Your throne will be a living throne, our loyal hearts; Your royal crown, our acts of love. O Mary, our Queen, by your loving submission to the will of God in all things, obtain for us the grace never to sadden the Heart of our King by willful disobedience to His Commandments or to those of His Church. May it be said of each of us what the Gospel says of Jesus, "He was obedient to them."

Good Saint Joseph, our guardian, help us to make our Enthronement the beginning of a new life of love for us. Through the presence of the Sacred Heart of Jesus, and through your powerful intercession, may we receive the grace to know our King more personally, love Him more ardently, and thus serve Him more faithfully. Amen.

INDULGENCED PRAYER

All: O Christ Jesus, I acknowledge You to be King of the universe; all that has been made is created by You. Exercise over me all Your sovereign rights. I hereby renew the promises of my Baptism, renouncing Satan and all his pomps and works, and I engage myself to lead henceforth a truly Christian life. And in a special manner do I undertake to bring about the triumph of the rights of God and His Church, so far as in me lies. Divine Heart of Jesus, I offer You my poor actions to obtain the acknowledgment by every heart of Your sacred kingly power. In such wisdom may the kingdom of Your peace be firmly established throughout all the earth.

Leader: Most Sacred Heart of Jesus,
R/. Thy Kingdom come through Mary.

Leader: Sacred Heart of Jesus,
R/. protect us.

Leader: Immaculate Heart of Mary, Queen of Heaven,
R/. pray for us.

Leader: Saint Joseph, friend of the Sacred Heart,
R/. pray for us.

Leader: Saint Michael, first champion of the Kingship of Christ,
R/. pray for us.

Leader: Guardian Angels,
R/. pray for us.

HYMN

Immaculate Mary

Melody is on page 175.

1. Immaculate Mary, thy praises we sing,
   Who reignest in splendor with Jesus our King.
   Ave, Ave, Ave María! Ave, Ave María!

2. In heaven the blessed thy glory proclaim,
   On earth we thy children invoke thy fair name.
   Ave, Ave, Ave María! Ave, Ave María!

3. Thy name is our power, thy virtues our light,
   Thy love is our comfort, thy pleading our might.
   Ave, Ave, Ave, María! Ave, Ave, María!

4. We pray for our Mother, the Church upon earth,
   And bless, sweetest Lady, the land of our birth.
   Ave, Ave, Ave Maria! Ave, Ave Maria!

THE SECOND DAY

To the Heart of Our Brother, Jesus of Nazareth

SIGN OF THE CROSS
Leader: In the name of the Father, and of the Son, and of the Holy Spirit.
R/. Amen.

SCRIPTURE READING
Leader: The Fifth Joyful Mystery, *The Finding of the Child Jesus in the Temple, and His Return to Nazareth.* This mystery inspires us to model the life of our family upon the Holy Family as we think of Jesus, the Son of God, living an ordinary life in the little home at Nazareth with Mary and Joseph. The care of Mary and Joseph for Jesus and His obedience to them are models for our relationships within the family as well as with others.

Someone other than the leader reads:
A reading from the Holy Gospel according to Luke.

And the child grew and became strong, filled with wisdom; and the favor of God was upon him. Now his parents went to Jerusalem every year at the feast of the Passover. And when he was twelve years old, they went up according to custom; and when the feast was ended, as they were returning, the boy Jesus stayed behind in Jerusalem. His parents did not know it, but supposing him to be in the company they went a day's journey, and they sought him among their kinsfolk and acquaintances; and when they did not find him, they returned to Jerusalem, seeking him.

After three days they found him in the temple, sitting among the teachers, listening to them and asking them questions; and all who heard him were amazed at his understanding and his answers. And when they saw him they were astonished; and his mother said to him, "Son, why have you treated us so? Behold, your father and I have been looking for you anxiously." And he said to them, "How is it that you sought me? Did you not know that I must be in my Father's house?" And they did not understand the saying which he spoke to them. And he went down with them and came to Nazareth, and was obedient to them; and his mother kept all these things in her heart. And Jesus increased in wisdom and in stature, and in favor with God and man. (Luke 2:40-52)

The Word of the Lord.
R/. Thanks be to God.

PRAYER
The Fifth Joyful Mystery
The Finding of the Child Jesus in the Temple

LITANY OF THE SACRED HEART

Leader: Lord, have mercy.
R/. Christ, have mercy.

Leader: Lord, have mercy. Christ, hear us.
R/. Christ, graciously hear us.

Leader: God, the Father of Heaven,
R/. have mercy on us.

Leader: God the Son, Redeemer of the world,
R/. have mercy on us.

Leader: God the Holy Spirit,
R/. have mercy on us.

Holy Trinity, one God,
R/. have mercy on us.

Heart of Jesus, Son of the eternal Father, **R/.**
Heart of Jesus, formed by the Holy Spirit in the womb of the Virgin Mother, **R/.**
Heart of Jesus, substantially united to the Word of God, **R/.**
Heart of Jesus, of infinite majesty, **R/.**
Heart of Jesus, sacred temple of God, **R/.**
Heart of Jesus, tabernacle of the Most High, **R/.**
Heart of Jesus, house of God and gate of Heaven, **R/.**
Heart of Jesus, burning furnace of charity, **R/.**
Heart of Jesus, abode of justice and love, **R/.**
Heart of Jesus, full of goodness and love, **R/.**
Heart of Jesus, abyss of all virtues, **R/.**
Heart of Jesus, most worthy of all praise, **R/.**
Heart of Jesus, King and center of all hearts, **R/.**
Heart of Jesus, in Whom are all the treasures of wisdom and knowledge, **R/.**
Heart of Jesus, in Whom dwells the fullness of divinity, **R/.**

Heart of Jesus, in Whom the Father was well pleased, **R/.**
Heart of Jesus, of Whose fullness we have all received, **R/.**
Heart of Jesus, desire of the everlasting hills, **R/.**
Heart of Jesus, patient and most merciful, **R/.**
Heart of Jesus, enriching all who invoke Thee, **R/.**
Heart of Jesus, fountain of life and holiness, **R/.**
Heart of Jesus, propitiation for our sins, **R/.**
Heart of Jesus, loaded down with opprobrium, **R/.**
Heart of Jesus, bruised for our offenses, **R/.**
Heart of Jesus, obedient unto death, **R/.**
Heart of Jesus, pierced with a lance, **R/.**
Heart of Jesus, source of all consolation, **R/.**
Heart of Jesus, our life and resurrection, **R/.**
Heart of Jesus, our peace and reconciliation, **R/.**
Heart of Jesus, victim for sin, **R/.**
Heart of Jesus, salvation of those who trust in Thee, **R/.**
Heart of Jesus, hope of those who die in Thee, **R/.**
Heart of Jesus, delight of all the saints, **R/.**

Leader: Lamb of God, Who takes away the sins of the world,
R/. spare us, O Lord.

Leader: Lamb of God, Who takes away the sins of the world,
R/. graciously hear us, O Lord.

Leader: Lamb of God, Who takes away the sins of the world,
R/. have mercy on us.

Leader: Jesus, meek and humble of Heart,
R/. make our hearts like unto Thine.

PRAYER

Leader: Let us pray. Dear Jesus, Son of God, when we call You "Brother," we speak the truth, for You are indeed just that. Saint John told us so when in his Gospel he wrote: "But to as many as received Him, He gave the power of becoming sons of God." Therefore we are Your adopted brothers and sisters and co-heirs of Heaven. But since You are a King, we too, have the privilege of being members of a royal family, as were Mary and Joseph.

How honored will we be to have our Brother-King come to dwell in our humble home in order to share our joys and sorrows! Once You are enthroned in our family, we will understand as never before the meaning of these words, "And the Word was made flesh and dwelt among us." No longer need we envy Mary and Joseph at Nazareth, for Your abiding presence in our home will make our family another Nazareth wherein we will vie with one another in giving You proofs of our love. We will do this especially by the practice of family charity, trying to love each other as You have loved us.

O Mary, Queen of Nazareth, Mother of Jesus, obtain for us the grace to appreciate the presence of your Divine Son enthroned in our home. Grant us a greater love for Jesus ever present in the Blessed Sacrament, a deeper love for Holy Mass, a more ardent longing to unite ourselves as often as possible with our loving Savior in Holy Communion.

Good Saint Joseph, you were privileged to share the joys and sorrows of your foster-Son at Nazareth. Teach us how to share our everyday joys and sorrows with our Brother Jesus, here on earth, so that one day our entire family may join Mary and you in sharing the joys of Heaven, where we will see our King and Brother face to face and, with you, love, adore, thank and praise Him for all eternity. Amen.

INDULGENCED PRAYER

All: O Christ Jesus, I acknowledge You to be King of the universe; all that has been made is created by You. Exercise over me all Your sovereign rights. I hereby renew the promises of my Baptism, renouncing Satan and all his pomps and works, and I engage myself to lead henceforth a truly Christian life. And in a special manner do I undertake to bring about the triumph of the rights of God and His Church, so far as in me lies. Divine Heart of Jesus, I offer You my poor actions to obtain the acknowledgment by every heart of Your sacred kingly power. In such wisdom may the kingdom of Your peace be firmly established throughout all the earth.

Leader: Eucharistic Heart of Jesus,
R/. Thy Kingdom come in our (*parish, school, or other setting*).

Leader: Our Lady of the Blessed Sacrament,
R/. pray for us.

Leader: Saint Joseph, foster-father of Our Lord Jesus Christ and true spouse of Mary the Virgin,
R/. pray for us.

Leader: Saints Joachim and Anne, parents of the Blessed Virgin Mary,
R/. pray for us.

Leader: Guardian Angels,
R/. pray for us.

HYMN

To Jesus Christ, Our Sov'reign King

Melody is on page 172.

1. To Jesus Christ, our Sov'reign King,
   Who is the world's salvation,
   All praise and homage do we bring,
   And thanks and adoration.

Refrain: Christ Jesus Victor...

2. Thy reign extend, O King benign,
   To ev'ry land and nation,
   For in Thy kingdom, Lord divine,
   Alone we find salvation.

Refrain: Christ Jesus Victor...

3. To Thee and to Thy Church, great King,
   We pledge our hearts' oblation,
   Until before Thy throne we sing,
   In endless jubilation.

Refrain: Christ Jesus Victor...

4. Thy majesty shall be the praise
   And thanks of ev'ry nation,
   To thee the world with joy shall raise
   The voice of exultation.

Refrain: Christ Jesus Victor...

5. May God the Father, God the Son,
   And God the Spirit bless us!
   Let all the world praise him alone,
   Let solemn awe possess us.

Refrain: Christ Jesus Victor...

THE THIRD DAY

To the Heart of Our Friend, Jesus of Bethany

SIGN OF THE CROSS

Leader: In the name of the Father, and of the Son, and of the Holy Spirit.
R/. Amen.

SCRIPTURE READING

Leader: The First Glorious Mystery, *The Resurrection.* Reflecting on this mystery helps us to recognize the living presence of Our Lord with us in the Church, and increases in us the desire to be with Him always. We think of Jesus rising in triumph from the tomb and hear Him promising Martha and Mary that their brother will rise again.

Someone other than the leader reads:

A reading from the Holy Gospel according to Luke.

Now a certain man was ill, Lazarus of Bethany, the village of Mary and her sister Martha. It was Mary who anointed the Lord with ointment and wiped his feet with her hair, whose brother Lazarus was ill. So the sisters sent to him, saying, "Lord, he whom you love is ill."

But when Jesus heard it he said, "This illness is not unto death; it is for the glory of God, so that the Son of God may be glorified by means of it." Now Jesus loved Martha and her sister and Lazarus. So when he heard that he was ill, he stayed two days longer in the place where he was. Then after this he said to the disciples, "Let us go into Judea again." The disciples said to him, "Rabbi, the Jews were but now seeking to stone you, and are you going there again?" Jesus answered, "Are there not twelve hours in the day? If any one walks in the day, he does not stumble, because he sees the light of this world. But if any one walks in the night, he stumbles, because the light is not in him." Thus he spoke, and then he said to them, "Our friend Lazarus has fallen asleep, but I go to awake him out of sleep." The disciples said to him, "Lord, if he has fallen asleep, he will recover." Now Jesus had spoken of his death, but they thought that he meant taking rest in sleep. Then Jesus told them plainly, "Lazarus is dead; and for your sake I am glad that I was not there, so that you may believe. But let us go to him." Thomas, called the Twin, said to his fellow disciples, "Let us also go, that we may die with him."

Now when Jesus came, he found that Lazarus had already been in the tomb four days. Bethany was near Jerusalem, about two miles off, and many of the Jews had come to Martha and Mary to console them concerning their brother. When Martha heard that Jesus was coming, she went and met him, while Mary sat in the house. Martha said to Jesus, "Lord, if you had been here, my brother would not have died. And even now I know that whatever you ask from God, God will give you." Jesus said to her, "Your brother will rise again." Martha said to him, "I know that he will rise again in the resurrection at the last day." Jesus said to her, "I am the resurrection and the life; he who believes in me, though he die, yet shall he live, and whoever lives and believes in me shall never die. Do you believe this?" She said to him, "Yes, Lord; I believe that you are the Christ, the Son of God, he who is coming into the world." (John 11:1-27)

The Word of the Lord.
R/. Thanks be to God.

PRAYER

The First Glorious Mystery
The Resurrection of Jesus

LITANY OF THE SACRED HEART

Leader: Lord, have mercy.
R/. Christ, have mercy.

Leader: Lord, have mercy. Christ, hear us.
R/. Christ, graciously hear us.

Leader: God, the Father of Heaven,
R/. have mercy on us.

Leader: God the Son, Redeemer of the world,
R/. have mercy on us.

Leader: God the Holy Spirit,
R/. have mercy on us.

Holy Trinity, one God,
R/. have mercy on us.

Heart of Jesus, Son of the eternal Father, **R/.**
Heart of Jesus, formed by the Holy Spirit in the womb of the Virgin Mother, **R/.**
Heart of Jesus, substantially united to the Word of God, **R/.**
Heart of Jesus, of infinite majesty, **R/.**
Heart of Jesus, sacred temple of God, **R/.**
Heart of Jesus, tabernacle of the Most High, **R/.**
Heart of Jesus, house of God and gate of Heaven, **R/.**
Heart of Jesus, burning furnace of charity, **R/.**
Heart of Jesus, abode of justice and love, **R/.**
Heart of Jesus, full of goodness and love, **R/.**
Heart of Jesus, abyss of all virtues, **R/.**
Heart of Jesus, most worthy of all praise, **R/.**
Heart of Jesus, King and center of all hearts, **R/.**
Heart of Jesus, in Whom are all the treasures of wisdom and knowledge, **R/.**
Heart of Jesus, in Whom dwells the fullness of divinity, **R/.**

Heart of Jesus, in Whom the Father was well pleased, **R/.**
Heart of Jesus, of Whose fullness we have all received, **R/.**
Heart of Jesus, desire of the everlasting hills, **R/.**
Heart of Jesus, patient and most merciful, **R/.**
Heart of Jesus, enriching all who invoke Thee, **R/.**
Heart of Jesus, fountain of life and holiness, **R/.**
Heart of Jesus, propitiation for our sins, **R/.**
Heart of Jesus, loaded down with opprobrium, **R/.**
Heart of Jesus, bruised for our offenses, **R/.**
Heart of Jesus, obedient unto death, **R/.**
Heart of Jesus, pierced with a lance, **R/.**
Heart of Jesus, source of all consolation, **R/.**
Heart of Jesus, our life and resurrection, **R/.**
Heart of Jesus, our peace and reconciliation, **R/.**
Heart of Jesus, victim for sin, **R/.**
Heart of Jesus, salvation of those who trust in Thee, **R/.**
Heart of Jesus, hope of those who die in Thee, **R/.**
Heart of Jesus, delight of all the saints, **R/.**

Leader: Lamb of God, Who takes away the sins of the world,
R/. spare us, O Lord.

Leader: Lamb of God, Who takes away the sins of the world,
R/. graciously hear us, O Lord.

Leader: Lamb of God, Who takes away the sins of the world,
R/. have mercy on us.

Leader: Jesus, meek and humble of Heart,
R/. make our hearts like unto Thine.

PRAYER

Leader: Let us pray. "My delights are to be with the children of men." These words from the *Book of Proverbs* were certainly spoken about You, dear Jesus, Who came down to share our exile here below. You delight in being with us because we need You and You are our best Friend. You love all without exception: saints and sinners, the rich and the poor, the learned and the uneducated. You love all races and all peoples, but, above all, you love all families. You proved that love by spending thirty years in Your home at Nazareth, and during Your public life, many times You accepted invitations to visit families. You even told Zacchaeus the sinner, "I must stay in thy house today."

But there was one family for whom You had a special love, that of Lazarus, Martha and Mary. How many times did You not stay with that beloved family at Bethany! It was there You found rest and solace after the fatigue of Your labors and the insulting attacks of Your enemies. At Bethany, You were always received as a royal Guest, but also You were treated as a Brother and a Friend.

Dear Jesus, once You are enthroned in our home, we, too, want to be Your true friends. We want You to feel at home with us. We will try to console You for those who do not love You. We will serve You like Martha, listen to You like Mary, and thank You as did Lazarus. We feel confident that You will richly bless our family as You did the family of Lazarus and all those families who invited You into their homes.

And if there are in our homes prodigal sons, lost sheep, sinners dead to the life of grace, we know that You will say to them as You did to Zacchaeus, "Today salvation has come to this house." You will be to them a loving Father, a Good Shepherd, a Divine Physician, for You are "the Resurrection and the Life."

O Mary, Mother of our best Friend, and Saint Joseph, our patron, obtain for us the grace to make our home a true Bethany of the Sacred Heart. May our friendship with Jesus be loving, loyal and lasting. May our daily living with our King and our Guest bring about a closer union of hearts, minds and wills so that our entire family, united with the Heart of Jesus here on earth, may remain united with Him and the Father and the Holy Spirit in our true home, Heaven, for all eternity! Amen.

INDULGENCED PRAYER

All: O Christ Jesus, I acknowledge You to be King of the universe; all that has been made is created by You. Exercise over me all Your sovereign rights. I hereby renew the promises of my Baptism, renouncing Satan and all his pomps and works, and I engage myself to lead henceforth a truly Christian life. And in a special manner do I undertake to bring about the triumph of the rights of God and His Church, so far as in me lies. Divine Heart of Jesus, I offer You my poor actions to obtain the acknowledgment by every heart of Your sacred kingly power. In such wisdom may the kingdom of Your peace be firmly established throughout all the earth.

Leader: Heart of Jesus, King, Brother and Friend of our family, we welcome You.
R/. Thy Kingdom come.

Leader: Our Lady of the Sacred Heart,
R/. pray for us.

Leader: Saint Joseph, model and patron of lovers of the Sacred Heart,
R/. pray for us.

Leader: Saints Lazarus, Martha, and Mary,
R/. pray for us.

Leader: Guardian Angels,
R/. pray for us.

Leader: O Jesus, Friend of little children,
R/. bless the little children of the whole world.

HYMN

Holy God, We Praise Thy Name

Melody is on page 174.

1. Holy God, we praise thy name!
Lord of all, we bow before thee!
All on Earth thy sceptre claim,
All in Heav'n above adore thee;
Infinite thy vast domain,
Everlasting is thy reign.

2. Hark! the loud celestial hymn
Angel choirs above are raising!
Cherubim and seraphim,
In unceasing chorus praising,
Fill the heav'ns with sweet accord;
Holy, holy, holy, Lord!

3. Lo! The blessed Twelve proclaim
To the Father hymns of glory;
Prophets sing in loud acclaim;
Martyrs tell the wondrous story;
And from morn to set of sun
Through the Church they sing as one.

4. Holy Father, Holy Son,
Holy Spirit, Three we name thee,
While in essence only One,
Undivided God we claim thee;
And adoring bend the knee,
While we own the mystery.

CEREMONY *for the* ENTHRONEMENT *of the* SACRED HEART IN PARISHES, CATHOLIC SCHOOLS, AND OTHER SETTINGS

The Enthronement is fittingly carried out in parishes, Catholic schools and other settings where every activity is directed to the Christian growth of parishioners, students, families and other members of the faithful. The Enthronement publicly proclaims the rule of the Heart of Jesus over the persons and activities of the place. It is an act of reparation for the offenses committed against His Heart and, by the ***Act of Consecration****, a pledge to honor the Sacred Heart now and in the future.*

Ideally, the Enthronement takes place in the context of the Holy Sacrifice of the Mass. After suitable preparation, the Enthronement is carried out by a priest and his parishioners, by a school's administrators and its staff, students and guests, or by members of any other Catholic community or organization.

OPTION A:

ENTHRONEMENT OUTSIDE OF HOLY MASS

The Enthronement Ceremony begins at a table on which the image of the Sacred Heart and holy water have been placed. This table should be somewhat distant from the place of Enthronement so that a procession may be formed to the place of Enthronement. The priest will bless the image during the Enthronement Ceremony, but if a priest is not present, the image should be blessed beforehand, and another figure of authority assumes the role of leader.

OPENING HYMN

To Jesus Christ, Our Sov'reign King
Melody is on page 172.

1. To Jesus Christ, our Sov'reign King,
Who is the world's salvation,
All praise and homage do we bring,
And thanks and adoration.

Refrain: Christ Jesus Victor...

2. Thy reign extend, O King benign,
To ev'ry land and nation,
For in Thy kingdom, Lord divine,
Alone we find salvation.

Refrain: Christ Jesus Victor...

3. To Thee and to Thy Church, great King,
We pledge our hearts' oblation,
Until before Thy throne we sing,
In endless jubilation.

Refrain: Christ Jesus Victor...

4. Thy majesty shall be the praise
And thanks of ev'ry nation,
To thee the world with joy shall raise
The voice of exultation.

Refrain: Christ Jesus Victor...

5. May God the Father, God the Son,
And God the Spirit bless us!
Let all the world praise him alone,
Let solemn awe possess us.

Refrain: Christ Jesus Victor...

SIGN OF THE CROSS

Leader: In the name of the Father, and of the Son, and of the Holy Spirit.
R/. Amen.

Leader: The Lord be with you.
R/. And with your spirit.

INTRODUCTION

Leader: "God is Love" (1 John 4:16), and all of His works serve to show this divine love to mankind. The writings of the Old Testament reveal that God's love created us in His image and likeness; it established a covenant with Abraham; it rescued the Chosen People from slavery in Egypt and brought them to the Promised Land. The fullest expression of God's love is the Person of Jesus Christ: "For God so loved the world that He gave His only-begotten Son, that whoever believes in Him should not perish but have eternal life" (*John* 3:16). The Heart of Jesus Itself, in love with and wounded for mankind, is the most perfect symbol of the love of God. For this reason, "The prayer of the Church venerates and honors the Heart of Jesus... It adores the Incarnate Word and His Heart which, out of love for men, He allowed to be pierced by our sins" (*Catechism of the Catholic Church*, n. 2669).

The Enthronement of the Sacred Heart of Jesus, for which we are gathered, is an expression of our own love of God and the love which He shows to us. The enthroned image of the Sacred Heart expresses the true Kingship of Christ Who rules over us by giving up His life for us. It daily reminds each of us to follow in Christ's royal way by making reparation for sins and striving to serve God and neighbor more lovingly.

The image of the Sacred Heart of Jesus is enthroned to signify that Christ is He Who gives inspiration and direction to each of us. The Enthronement is a single act, but it represents a way of life by which each of us is transformed in Christ each day.

May the Enthronement truly be for us a source of new vigor in living the Christian vocation, the vocation to love.

APOSTLES' CREED

Leader: As an act of loving faith in all of Jesus' teachings, and as an act of atonement for those who reject them or do not practice them, let us recite the Apostles' Creed together.

All: I believe in God, the Father Almighty,
Creator of Heaven and earth;
and in Jesus Christ, His only Son, Our Lord;
Who was conceived by the Holy Spirit,
born of the Virgin Mary,
suffered under Pontius Pilate, was crucified, died, and was buried.
He descended into Hell;
the third day He arose again from the dead.
He ascended into Heaven, and sits at the right hand of God, the Father Almighty;
from thence He shall come to judge the living and the dead.

I believe in the Holy Spirit,
the Holy Catholic Church,
the Communion of Saints, the forgiveness of sins,
the resurrection of the body and life everlasting.
Amen.

SCRIPTURE READING

Someone other than the leader reads:

A reading from the First Letter of John.

Beloved, let us love one another; for love is of God, and he who loves is born of God and knows God. He who does not love does not know God; for God is love. In this the love of God was made manifest among us, that God sent his only-begotten Son into the world, so that we might live through him. In this is love, not that we loved God but that he loved us and sent his Son to be the expiation for our sins.

Beloved, if God so loved us, we also ought to love one another. No man has ever seen God; if we love one another, God abides in us and his love is perfected in us. By this we know that we abide in him and he in us, because he has given us of his own Spirit. And we have seen and testify that the Father has sent his Son as the Savior of the world. Whoever confesses that Jesus is the Son of God, God abides in him, and he in God. So we know and believe the love God has for us. (1 *John* 4:7-16a)

The Word of the Lord.
R/. Thanks be to God.

Other readings may be used, particularly the account of the Annunciation (Luke 1:26-33), Our Lord's meeting with Zacchaeus (Luke 19:1-10) or Our Lord's visit to the home of Martha and Mary (Luke 10:38-41).

REFLECTION (optional)
A brief reflection may be offered by the leader.

BLESSING OF THE IMAGE

The image of the Sacred Heart is to be blessed by a priest. If an image of the Immaculate Heart of Mary is installed, the blessing found on page 143 may be used. If the images were previously blessed, the blessings are omitted at this time.

Priest:
Lord,
although Your glory lies beyond our sight,
out of Your great love
You have revealed Yourself in the Heart of Christ.
Bless [*sprinkle holy water*] this image of Your Son.
May those who venerate it
honor Christ by growing in His likeness,
Who is Lord for ever and ever.

R/. Amen.

The priest sprinkles the image with holy water.

ACT OF ENTHRONEMENT

For the procession, an incense bearer, cross and candle bearers, the leader carrying the image of the Sacred Heart, and a person carrying the Bible are followed by the parishioners, school community, or other members of the faithful. All process to the place of Enthronement. A hymn may accompany the procession.

When all arrive at the place of Enthronement, the leader enthrones the image of the Sacred Heart in the selected place saying:

I now enthrone Jesus as King and Friend of our (parish, school, or other setting).

The person carrying the Bible then places it near the image of the Sacred Heart and says:

We are nourished by the Body and Blood of Christ, and by the Word of God.

The candles are then placed on either side of the image as the candle bearers say together:

The Lord sits enthroned as King forever! (*Psalm* 29:10b)
All that the Lord has spoken we will do, and we will be obedient. (*Exodus* 24:7)

If incense is used, the image is incensed.

ACT OF CONSECRATION

If possible, all kneel and say in unison:

To the Sacred Heart of Our Lord, Jesus Christ, we give ourselves and consecrate our lives, our actions, pains, and sufferings, so that we may be unwilling to make use of any part of our being other than to honor, love, and glorify Your Sacred Heart.

This is our unchanging purpose, namely, to be all Yours and to do all things for the love of You, at the same time renouncing with all our hearts whatever is displeasing to You. We therefore take You, O Sacred Heart, to be the only object of our love, the guardian of our lives, our assurance of salvation, the remedy of our weakness, the atonement for all our faults, and our sure refuge at the hour of death.

Be then, O Heart of goodness, our justification before God the Father. O Heart of love, we put all our confidence in You, for we fear everything from our own weakness and frailty, but we hope for all things from Your goodness and bounty.

Remove from us all that can displease You or resist Your Holy Will; let Your pure love imprint Your image so deeply upon our hearts that we shall never be able to forget You or to be separated from You.

May we obtain from Your loving kindness the grace of having our names written in Your Heart, for in You we desire to place all our happiness and glory, living and dying in You, Who live and reign with the Father and the Holy Spirit, one God, for ever and ever. Amen.

If an image of the Immaculate Heart of Mary is installed, the ***Act of Consecration to the Immaculate Heart*** *found on page 143 is made at this point.*

INTERCESSIONS

Leader: Lord Jesus, You told us that "whatever you ask the Father in my name, he will give to you." In Your name, and with great confidence in Your love, we now offer these prayers:

Someone other than the leader proposes the intercessions:

For the grace of being faithful to this covenant with Jesus and our renewed way of life in Him, let us pray:
R/. Lord, hear our prayer.

For an increase of personal, generous love for Jesus, and a greater trust in His merciful love, let us pray:
R/. Lord, hear our prayer.

That the Holy Spirit may always find our hearts responsive to His call, let us pray:
R/. Lord, hear our prayer.

For a deeper appreciation of the greatest gift of the Heart of Jesus, the Holy Eucharist, through frequent participation in the Holy Sacrifice of the Mass and Holy Communion, especially on First Fridays, let us pray:
R/. Lord, hear our prayer.

That we may desire to receive the Sacrament of Confession more often in order to increase our love for Jesus and to avoid sin, let us pray:
R/. Lord, hear our prayer.

That those who are absent may be protected in all they do, and that all our beloved who have died may be united to the Heart of Jesus in Heaven for ever, let us pray:
R/. Lord, hear our prayer.

Leader:
God our Father,
through the Sacred Heart of Your Son, Jesus,
You pour forth Your eternal love upon us.
By the enthronement of the image of Jesus' Heart
and our consecration to It,
may we show our love to You and to the world.
We ask this through the same Christ Our Lord.

R/. Amen.

Leader: Let us conclude by calling on the Mother of God, Mary Most Holy:

HAIL HOLY QUEEN

All: Hail, Holy Queen, Mother of Mercy, our life, our sweetness, and our hope! To thee do we cry, poor banished children of Eve; to thee do we send up our sighs, mourning and weeping in this valley of tears. Turn then, most gracious advocate, thine eyes of mercy toward us, and after this our exile, show unto us the blessed fruit of thy womb, Jesus. O clement, O loving, O sweet Virgin Mary.

Leader: Pray for us, O holy Mother of God.
R/. That we may be made worthy of the promises of Christ.

Leader: Most Sacred Heart of Jesus,
R/. have mercy on us.

Leader: Immaculate Heart of Mary,
R/. pray for us!

Leader: Saint Joseph,
R/. pray for us!

Leader: Our Guardian Angels,
R/. pray for us!

Leader: Most Sacred Heart of Jesus,
R/. have mercy on us.

CLOSING PRAYER

Leader: Let us pray. O Father of mercies and God of all consolation, Who by the exceeding love with which You have loved us, have given us the Heart of Your beloved Son so that having but one heart with Him, we may love You perfectly, grant, we beseech You, that our hearts, being consumed in unity with the Heart of Jesus and with one another, may perform all our works in accord with His humility and charity and that, by His mediation, the just desires of our hearts may be accomplished, through the same Christ Our Lord.
R/. Amen.

If a priest is present, the Rite of Enthronement concludes with a blessing. Otherwise, the Rite concludes with the ***Sign of the Cross****.*

BLESSING AND DISMISSAL

Priest: The Lord be with you.
R/. And with your spirit.

Priest: May almighty God bless you,
the Father, the Son, and [*sprinkle holy water*] the Holy Spirit.
R/. Amen.

Priest: Go in peace.
R/. Thanks be to God.

CLOSING HYMN

Holy God, We Praise Thy Name

Melody is on page 174.

1. Holy God, we praise thy name!
Lord of all, we bow before thee!
All on Earth thy sceptre claim,
All in Heav'n above adore thee;
Infinite thy vast domain,
Everlasting is thy reign.

2. Hark! the loud celestial hymn
Angel choirs above are raising!
Cherubim and seraphim,
In unceasing chorus praising,
Fill the heav'ns with sweet accord;
Holy, holy, holy, Lord!

3. Lo! The blessed Twelve proclaim
To the Father hymns of glory;
Prophets sing in loud acclaim;
Martyrs tell the wondrous story;
And from morn to set of sun
Through the Church they sing as one.

4. Holy Father, Holy Son,
Holy Spirit, Three we name thee,
While in essence only One,
Undivided God we claim thee;
And adoring bend the knee,
While we own the mystery.

The ***Certificate of Enthronement*** *found on page 179 may be downloaded and signed at this time.*

OPTION B:
ENTHRONEMENT DURING HOLY MASS

The Enthronement is to take place following the Prayer After Communion, at which time the congregation will process to the place of Enthronement.

The image of the Sacred Heart is to be blessed at the end of the intercessions. The following intercessions are recommended:

INTERCESSIONS

Priest: Lord Jesus, You told us that "whatever you ask the Father in my name, he will give to you." In Your name, and with great confidence in Your love, we now offer these prayers:

Someone other than the celebrant proposes the intercessions:

For the grace of being faithful to this covenant with Jesus and our renewed way of life in Him, let us pray:
R/. Lord, hear our prayer.

For an increase of personal, generous love for Jesus, and a greater trust in His merciful love, let us pray:
R/. Lord, hear our prayer.

That the Holy Spirit may always find our hearts responsive to His call, let us pray:
R/. Lord, hear our prayer.

For a deeper appreciation of the greatest gift of the Heart of Jesus, the Holy Eucharist, through frequent participation in the Holy Sacrifice of the Mass and Holy Communion, especially on First Fridays, let us pray:
R/. Lord, hear our prayer.

That we may desire to receive the Sacrament of Confession more often in order to increase our love for Jesus and to avoid sin, let us pray:
R/. Lord, hear our prayer.

That those who are absent may be protected in all they do, and that all our beloved who have died may be united to the Heart of Jesus in Heaven for ever, let us pray:
R/. Lord, hear our prayer.

BLESSING OF THE IMAGE

The image of the Sacred Heart is blessed by the priest. If an image of the Immaculate Heart of Mary is installed, the blessing found on page 143 may be used. If the images were previously blessed, the blessings are omitted at this time.

Priest:
Lord, although Your glory lies beyond our sight, out of Your great love You have revealed Yourself in the Heart of Christ. Bless [*sprinkle holy water*] this image of Your Son. May those who venerate it
honor Christ by growing in His likeness, Who is Lord for ever and ever.

R/. Amen.

The priest sprinkles the image with holy water.

ACT OF ENTHRONEMENT

Following the Prayer After Communion, a procession forms. An incense bearer, cross and candle bearers, the person carrying the image of the Sacred Heart, and a person carrying the Bible are followed by the priest and other ministers, then the members of the particular community. All process to the place of Enthronement. A hymn may accompany the procession.

When all arrive at the place of Enthronement, the priest enthrones the image of the Sacred Heart in the selected place saying:

I now enthrone Jesus as King and Friend of our (parish, school, or other setting).

The person carrying the Bible then places it near the image of the Sacred Heart and says:

We are nourished by the Body and Blood of Christ, and by the Word of God.

The candles are then placed on either side of the image as the candle bearers say together:

The Lord sits enthroned as King forever! (Psalm 29:10b) All that the Lord has spoken we will do, and we will be obedient. (Exodus 24:7)

If incense is used, the image is incensed.

ACT OF CONSECRATION

If possible, all kneel and say in unison:

To the Sacred Heart of Our Lord, Jesus Christ, we give ourselves and consecrate our lives, our actions, pains, and sufferings, so that we may be unwilling to make use of any part of our being other than to honor, love, and glorify Your Sacred Heart.

This is our unchanging purpose, namely, to be all Yours and to do all things for the love of You, at the same time renouncing with all our hearts whatever is displeasing to You. We therefore take You, O Sacred Heart, to be the only object of our love, the guardian of our lives, our assurance of salvation, the remedy of our weakness, the atonement for all our faults, and our sure refuge at the hour of death.

Be then, O Heart of goodness, our justification before God the Father. O Heart of love, we put all our confidence in You, for we fear everything from our own weakness and frailty, but we hope for all things from Your goodness and bounty.

Remove from us all that can displease You or resist Your Holy Will; let Your pure love imprint Your image so deeply upon our hearts that we shall never be able to forget You or to be separated from You.

May we obtain from Your loving kindness the grace of having our names written in Your Heart, for in You we desire to place all our happiness and glory, living and dying in You, Who live and reign with the Father and the Holy Spirit, one God, for ever and ever. Amen.

If an image of the Immaculate Heart of Mary is installed, the Act of Consecration to the Immaculate Heart found on page 143 is made at this point.

Priest: Let us conclude by calling on the Mother of God, Mary Most Holy:

HAIL HOLY QUEEN

All: Hail, Holy Queen, Mother of Mercy, our life, our sweetness, and our hope! To thee do we cry, poor banished children of Eve; to thee do we send up our sighs, mourning and weeping in this valley of tears. Turn then, most gracious advocate, thine eyes of mercy toward us, and after this our exile, show unto us the blessed fruit of thy womb, Jesus. O clement, O loving, O sweet Virgin Mary.

Priest: Pray for us, O holy Mother of God.
R/. That we may be made worthy of the promises of Christ.

Priest: Most Sacred Heart of Jesus,
R/. have mercy on us.

Leader: Immaculate Heart of Mary,
R/. pray for us!

Leader: Saint Joseph,
R/. pray for us!

Leader: Our Guardian Angels,
R/. pray for us!

Priest: Most Sacred Heart of Jesus,
R/. have mercy on us.

CLOSING PRAYER

Priest: Let us pray. O Father of mercies and God of all consolation, Who by the exceeding love with which You have loved us, have given us the Heart of Your beloved Son so that having but one heart with Him, we may love You perfectly, grant, we beseech You, that our hearts, being consumed in unity with the Heart of Jesus and with one another, may perform all our works in accord with His humility and charity and that, by His mediation, the just desires of our hearts may be accomplished, through the same Christ Our Lord.

R/. Amen.

BLESSING AND DISMISSAL

Priest: The Lord be with you.
R/. And with your spirit.

Priest: May almighty God bless you, the Father, the Son, and [*sprinkle holy water*] the Holy Spirit.
R/. Amen.

Priest: Go in peace.
R/. Thanks be to God.

CLOSING HYMN

Holy God, We Praise Thy Name

Melody is on page 174.

1. Holy God, we praise thy name!
   Lord of all, we bow before thee!
   All on Earth thy sceptre claim,
   All in Heav'n above adore thee;
   Infinite thy vast domain,
   Everlasting is thy reign.

2. Hark! the loud celestial hymn
   Angel choirs above are raising!
   Cherubim and seraphim,
   In unceasing chorus praising,
   Fill the heav'ns with sweet accord;
   Holy, holy, holy, Lord!

3. Lo! The blessed Twelve proclaim
   To the Father hymns of glory;
   Prophets sing in loud acclaim;
   Martyrs tell the wondrous story;
   And from morn to set of sun
   Through the Church they sing as one.

4. Holy Father, Holy Son,
   Holy Spirit, Three we name thee,
   While in essence only One,
   Undivided God we claim thee;
   And adoring bend the knee,
   While we own the mystery.

The ***Certificate of Enthronement*** *found on page 179 may be downloaded and signed at this time.*

CONSECRATION *to the* IMMACULATE HEART *of* MARY BLESSING OF THE IMAGE *of the* IMMACULATE HEART

When the Immaculate Heart of Mary is installed, the image is to be blessed by a priest. The blessing is omitted at the time of Enthronement if the image has already been blessed.

Priest:
Lord, in the Blessed Virgin Mary
You have given Your pilgrim Church an image of the glory to come.
Bless [*sprinkle holy water*] this image
of the Blessed Virgin Mary,
Mother of Our Lord Jesus Christ.
Grant, we beseech Thee,
that those who honor her Immaculate Heart in this image
may humbly strive to serve and honor
Your only-begotten Son, Our Lord Jesus Christ.
Through the intercession of the Blessed Virgin Mary,
may they gain from You grace in the present life and
eternal glory in the life to come, through Christ Our Lord.
R/. Amen.

The priest sprinkles the image with holy water.

ACT OF CONSECRATION TO THE IMMACULATE HEART

All: Most Holy Virgin Mary, tender Mother of men, to fulfill the desires of the Sacred Heart of Jesus and the request of the Vicar of your Son on earth, we consecrate ourselves and our families to your Sorrowful and Immaculate Heart, O Queen of the Most Holy Rosary, and we recommend to you, all the people of our country and all the world.

Please accept our Consecration, dearest Mother, and use us as you wish to accomplish your designs in the world.

O Sorrowful and Immaculate Heart of Mary, Queen of the Most Holy Rosary, and Queen of the World, rule over us, together with the Sacred Heart of Jesus Christ, Our King. Save us from the spreading flood of modern paganism; kindle in our hearts and homes the love of purity, the practice of a virtuous life, an ardent zeal for souls, and a desire to pray the Rosary more faithfully.

We come with confidence to you, O Throne of Grace and Mother of Fair Love. Inflame us with the same Divine Fire which has inflamed your own Sorrowful and Immaculate Heart. Make our hearts and homes your shrine, and through us, make the Heart of Jesus, together with your rule, triumph in every heart and home. Amen. (Venerable Pope Pius XII)

Enthronement prayers continue with the INTERCESSIONS on the following pages:

- *For Enthronement in the Home, page 87;*

For Enthronement in Parishes, Schools and Other Settings

- *outside of Holy Mass, page 130;*
- *during Holy Mass, page 136.*

PRAYERS

O Sacred Heart of Jesus, formed by the Holy Spirit in the womb of the Virgin Mother, have mercy on us.

MORNING OFFERING *to the* SACRED HEART OF JESUS

O Jesus, through the Immaculate Heart of Mary, I offer You my prayers, works, joys, and sufferings of this day in union with the Holy Sacrifice of the Mass throughout the world. I offer them for all the intentions of Your Sacred Heart: the salvation of souls, reparation for sin, the reunion of all Christians; I offer them for the intentions of our Bishops and of all Apostles of Prayer, and in particular for those recommended by our Holy Father this month. Amen.

Daily Prayer *to the* Sacred Heart of Jesus

Dear Sacred Heart of Jesus, we renew our pledge of love and loyalty to You. Keep us always close to Your loving Heart and to the most pure Heart of Your Mother.

May we love one another more and more each day, forgiving each other's faults as You forgive us our sins. Teach us to see You in the members of our family and those we meet outside our home, and to love them, especially the poor and oppressed, that we may be instrumental in bringing about justice and peace.

Please help us to carry our cross daily out of love for You, and to strengthen this love by frequent Holy Mass and Holy Communion.

Thank You, dear Jesus, King and Friend of our family, for all the blessings of this day. Protect us and all families during this night. Help us so to live that we may all get to Heaven.

Most Sacred Heart of Jesus, have mercy on us.

Immaculate Heart of Mary, pray for us!

Saint Joseph, pray for us!!

Our Guardian Angels, pray for us!

Most Sacred Heart of Jesus, have mercy on us.

ACT *of* RENEWAL

*This prayer, or the **Act of Consecration** on page 85, may be used to renew your Consecration on the Feast of the Sacred Heart, First Fridays, birthdays, anniversaries, or in times of sickness or death. It may also be used daily.*

Most kind Jesus, humbly kneeling at Thy feet, we renew our Consecration to Thy Divine Heart. Be Thou our King forever! In Thee we have full and entire confidence. May Thy Spirit penetrate our thoughts, our desires, our words and our deeds. Bless our undertakings; share in our joys, in our trials and in our daily labors. Grant us to know Thee better, to love Thee more, to serve Thee without faltering.

By the Immaculate Heart of Mary, Queen of Peace, set up Thy Kingdom in our country. Enter closely into the midst of our families and make them Thine own through the solemn Enthronement of Thy Sacred Heart, so that soon one cry may resound from home to home: “May the triumphant Heart of Jesus be everywhere loved, blessed and glorified forever!” Honor and glory to the Sacred Hearts of Jesus and Mary.

Sacred Heart of Jesus, protect our families.

Most Sacred Heart of Jesus, Thy Kingdom come!

Immaculate Heart of Mary, pray for us!

Saint Joseph, friend of the Sacred Heart, pray for us! Our Patron Saints and Guardian Angels, pray for us!

The HOLY ROSARY

A METHOD OF PRAYER[58]

The method of prayer of the Rosary is the repetition of words which express our deep love of God. It is not a tedious exercise but rather the repeated expression of deep love. We never tire of the words, and we never tire of repeating them, because through them we draw ever closer to God Whom we love with all our heart. The goal of the method is our ever deeper appreciation of and union with the mystery of God's love for us, upon which we meditate.

The very form of the prayer underlines the mystery of the Incarnation. God has taken a human heart, now the glorious Heart of Jesus seated at the right hand of the Father, which receives with great affection our repeated expressions of love. In his Apostolic Letter, *Rosarium Virginis Mariae*, Pope Saint John Paul II recalls to our mind how Christ asked Peter three times: "Do you love me?" Christ's repeated question and Saint Peter's repeated response help us to understand the beauty of praying the Rosary as a repeated response of our love for God.[59]

---

[58] Originally published in 2003 and is now available on the website of the Marian Catechist Apostolate, "Commentary on *Rosarium Virginis Mariae*: Sitting at the School of Mary," mariancatechist.com/blog/commentary-on-rosarium-virginis-mariae/

The repetition is centered principally upon the Hail Mary, addressed to Mary. But the prayer is directed, with Mary and through her intercession, to her divine Son, our Lord Jesus. It expresses our desire to be ever more fully united to Christ, to become ever more Christlike. Ultimately, the Rosary is a most wonderful expression of the daily conversion of life by which we grow in holiness.

The method of the Rosary respects our human nature and engages our whole being in prayer. The Rosary expresses our perseverance in seeking Christ above all. As the Holy Father observes, it "embodies the desire for Christ to become the breath, the soul and the 'all' of one's life."[60]

Our Holy Father notes that the Rosary responds very well to a contemporary interest in meditative prayer, which frequently seeks satisfaction in the practices of other religions, practices which may be based on beliefs contrary to our faith. The Rosary helps us to achieve the meditation desired in a manner which corresponds perfectly to our Catholic faith.[61]

The method of the Rosary, effective as it has been over the centuries and continues to be, certainly can be improved. For instance, the Holy Father has added five new mysteries to make fuller our meditation upon the mystery of Christ's life in us. The Holy Father also makes a number of other suggestions in order to help us to pray the Rosary more effectively.

---

[59] John Paul II, "Rosarium Virginis Mariae" (English) (Vatican City: Libreria Editrice Vaticana, 2014), 26.

[60] John Paul II, "Rosarium Virginis Mariae," 27.

[61] John Paul II, "Rosarium Virginis Mariae," 28a.

SUGGESTIONS FOR PRAYING THE ROSARY

The first suggestion is the use of a sacred image to announce each mystery. Through an icon or other sacred image, our mind and heart is directed more fully to the "particular episode or moment in the life of Christ."[62] Once again, the care to engage the imagination in announcing each mystery respects the truth of the Incarnation: God has come to us in our human nature. Regarding the announcement of each mystery, the Holy Father reminds us that the Rosary does not replace the meditative reading of the Holy Scriptures (*Lectio Divina*) but rather stirs up the desire for meditation upon the Word of God and flows from such meditation. The Rosary is a continuing meditation upon the Holy Scriptures throughout the day.[63]

The second suggestion of the Holy Father, therefore, is to follow the announcement of each mystery with "the proclamation of a related Biblical passage," which can be shorter or longer, depending upon the situation. The proclamation of familiar texts of the Word of God greatly assists in the assimilation of the mysteries of our faith through the Rosary. "It is not a matter of recalling information but of allowing God to speak."[64]

The third suggestion is to observe a period of silence after the announcement of each mystery and the proclamation of the relevant passage from the Bible. Silence helps us to focus upon the mystery about which we are about to meditate. Silence helps us to put out the distractions which keep us from praying fervently.[65]

---

[62] John Paul II, "Rosarium Virginis Mariae," 29.
[63] cf. John Paul II, "Rosarium Virginis Mariae," 29.
[64] John Paul II, "Rosarium Virginis Mariae," 30.
[65] cf. John Paul II, "Rosarium Virginis Mariae," 31.

THE PARTS OF THE ROSARY

The opening and closing of the praying of the Rosary vary from place to place. In our country, we have the most fitting practice of beginning the Rosary by praying the Apostles Creed. The profession of faith is the foundation of the meditation we undertake in praying the Rosary.[66]

The Rosary is concluded by saying an Our Father, Hail Mary, and Glory Be for the intentions of our Holy Father. In this way, the prayer of the Rosary embraces the needs of the universal Church. In order to encourage such truly Catholic prayer, the Church grants indulgences for the praying of the Rosary. Finally, we conclude the Rosary in which Mary is our "Mother, Teacher and Guide," by praising the Mother of God in the words of the Hail Holy Queen and/or the Litany of Loreto.[67]

We begin the meditation upon each mystery by praying the Our Father. Meditating upon the mysteries of the life of Christ, Christ draws us always closer to God the Father. By praying the Our Father, we express the ultimate goal of the praying of the Rosary: union with Christ in loving God the Father and in doing His will in all things.[68]

The Hail Mary is, as the Holy Father states, "the most substantial element in the Rosary."[69] It is a prayer to Mary, through which Mary leads us to Christ. The first part of the Hail Mary expresses adoration before the mystery of the Incarnation, accomplished with the cooperation of the Virgin Mary. The repetition of these words deepens our

---

[66] cf. John Paul II, "Rosarium Virginis Mariae," 32.
[67] cf. John Paul II, "Rosarium Virginis Mariae," 37.
[68] cf. John Paul II, "Rosarium Virginis Mariae," 32.
[69] John Paul II, "Rosarium Virginis Mariae," 33.

wonder at God's immeasurable love for us. The "center of gravity" or "the hinge" of the Hail Mary is the name of Jesus. The whole purpose of the Rosary is to have Mary help us to speak the name of Jesus with love, to welcome Christ ever more fully into our lives. The Holy Father reminds us of a method used in some places to highlight the "center of gravity," that is adding after the name of Jesus some words referring to the mystery. The third and last part of the Hail Mary is our appeal to her, entrusting to her loving intercession every moment of our life and the hour of our death.[70]

The Glory Be expresses the reality of our share in the life of the Holy Trinity, which we experience in praying the Rosary: the Incarnate Son leading us to the Father in the Holy Spirit. As the Holy Father aptly observes, it expresses the raising of our minds and hearts to Heaven, accomplished through the praying of the Rosary. Therefore, he suggests that it could be fittingly sung.[71]

The concluding prayer to each mystery varies. The Holy Father suggests that it would be good to conclude with a short prayer asking for the greater assimilation of the particular mystery in one's life, and expresses the hope that formulas of such concluding prayers for each mystery will be developed for the use of us all.[72]

---

[70] cf. John Paul II, "Rosarium Virginis Mariae," 33.
[71] cf. John Paul II, "Rosarium Virginis Mariae," 34.
[72] cf. John Paul II, "Rosarium Virginis Mariae," 35.

DISTRIBUTION OF THE MYSTERIES

While it is laudable to pray all of the mysteries of the Rosary every day, most of us must limit ourselves to praying one set of the mysteries. The Holy Father suggests the following distribution of the praying of the mysteries during each week: the Glorious Mysteries on Sunday and Wednesday; the Joyful Mysteries on Monday and Saturday; the Sorrowful Mysteries on Tuesday and Friday; and the Luminous Mysteries on Thursday. Clearly, particular circumstances, for instance the observance of a particular feast like the Annunciation, can justify the praying of the mysteries on days other than suggested.[73]

THE JOYFUL MYSTERIES

The first five decades of the Rosary are the Joyful Mysteries which invite us to reflect more deeply on the mystery of the Incarnation, the mystery of God's immeasurable love for us by which He has indeed become man in order to suffer and die for our salvation. The first mystery, the Annunciation, recalls the waiting of the People of God over many centuries for the coming of the Redeemer. When Mary replied "Yes" to the will of God that she become the Mother of the Redeemer, she spoke for all men and women of every time and every place, welcoming the long-awaited Redeemer.

The Visitation and the Nativity express the profound joy and gladness at God's coming in our human flesh. The

---

[73] John Paul II, "Rosarium Virginis Mariae," 38.

beautiful exclamation of Elizabeth and the leaping of John the Baptist in her womb reflect the mystery: "Blest is she who trusted that the Lord's words to her would be fulfilled."[74] In the scene of the Birth of our Lord, every detail underlines the wonder of the event heralded by angels to shepherds keeping watch by night.

The last two joyful mysteries point to the reason for the Incarnation, the mission upon which God the Father sent His Son into the world. They lead us to reflect upon both the joy of Christ's coming into the world and the profound sorrow of His suffering and dying. Simeon not only rejoices to see fulfilled the hope of the Messiah, but he also identifies Christ as "the sign of contradiction" and speaks of the "sword" of sorrow which will pierce the heart of His virgin Mother.[75]

The Holy Father tells us: "To meditate upon the 'joyful' mysteries, then, is to enter into the ultimate causes and the deepest meaning of Christian joy."[76] In the Joyful Mysteries, we look upon the Face of Christ, God become man for our redemption.

THE MYSTERIES OF LIGHT

In the five new mysteries proposed by the Holy Father, we contemplate the Face of Christ as He reveals God's love through His public ministry. The new mysteries are: 1) the Baptism in the Jordan; 2) the Wedding at Cana; 3) the

---

[74] Luke 1:15

[75] Luke 2:35

[76] John Paul II, "Rosarium Virginis Mariae," 20.

Proclamation of the Kingdom of God; 4) the Transfiguration; and 5) the Institution of the Holy Eucharist. In each of the luminous mysteries, as the Holy Father points out, we view the Kingdom of God in the person of the Redeemer.[77]

At His Baptism, God the Father declares the vocation and mission of His beloved Son, while the Holy Spirit descends upon Him in all His fullness for the carrying out of His mission. At the Wedding Feast of Cana, Christ performed the first of His saving signs, through the intercession of His Mother, revealing the tender mercy of God toward us. By the proclamation of the Kingdom of God, Christ calls all men and women to conversion and offers forgiveness to the contrite of heart. This mystery leads us to reflect in a special way upon the Sacrament of Penance by which Christ continuously calls us to conversion of life and grants the forgiveness of our sins.

The fourth mystery presents for our contemplation the glorious Christ on Mount Tabor, preparing us for His Passion and Death, so that we may share in His Resurrection, the outpouring of the Holy Spirit into our lives. The fifth mystery of light or luminous mystery is the Lord's Supper by which Christ renews for all time the outpouring of His life for us on Calvary.

Our Holy Father notes that our Blessed Mother "remains in the background" in these mysteries. Yet, even as witnessed at the Wedding of Cana, Mary was the first and best of the disciples of her divine Son. As the Holy Father indicates, her words at Cana, "Do whatever he tells you,"[78] reflect her discipleship, her accompanying us in the contemplation of Christ through the mysteries of light.

---

[77] cf. John Paul II, "Rosarium Virginis Mariae," 2.

[78] John 2:5

THE SORROWFUL MYSTERIES

The Incarnation comes to its fullness in the events by which our Lord suffered and died for our salvation. Through the Sorrowful Mysteries, we are invited to contemplate the face of Christ Who brings to completion His saving work. Each mystery, beginning with the Agony in the Garden, uncovers for us the great price which Christ paid for our salvation: the Scourging at the Pillar, the Crowning with Thorns, the Carrying of the Cross and the Crucifixion. The Sorrowful Mysteries make dramatically clear the immensity of God's love for us. At the same time, they reveal to us the mystery of our own life, the finding of our life by dying to self.

In the Sorrowful Mysteries, we stand with Mary at the foot of the cross and receive, with her, into our arms the lifeless body of her Son Who has given up His life for us. Through the contemplation of the Face of the sorrowful Christ, we find, with Mary, the life of God, offered for our eternal salvation.

THE GLORIOUS MYSTERIES

Through the Glorious Mysteries, we contemplate the Face of Christ Who has conquered sin and everlasting death. We find in them the cause of our faith, the sure anchor of our hope. We look upon the glorious Face of Christ in the Resurrection and Ascension. In the Descent of the Holy Spirit, we contemplate the abiding presence of the glorious Christ, now seated at the right hand of the Father, in the Church. Our Holy Father reminds us: "The contemplation of this scene, like that of the other glorious mysteries, ought to lead the faithful to an ever greater appreciation of their new life in Christ, lived in the heart of the Church, a life in which the scene of Pentecost itself is the great 'icon.'"[79]

In the fourth mystery, the Assumption, we contemplate our destiny which is sharing in the glory of Christ at the resurrection of the dead, which final destiny Mary was privileged to enjoy beforehand. In the fifth mystery, the Crowning of Mary as Queen of Heaven and Earth, we contemplate the Face of the glorious Christ in the fullness of life to which the whole Church is called in Him.

CONCLUDING THOUGHTS

Each mystery of the Rosary leads us to a deeper knowledge and love of Christ. They do not exhaust the mystery of His person but they surely lead us to know Him and to serve Him. The Rosary is, to use our Holy Father's words, "Mary's way": faith, silence and attentive listening. "By making our own the words of the Angel Gabriel and Saint Elizabeth contained in the Hail Mary, we find ourselves constantly drawn to seek out afresh in Mary, in her arms and in her heart, the 'blessed fruit of her womb.'"[80] The praying of the Rosary "marks the rhythm of human life."[81] Contemplating the Face of Christ in the mysteries of the Holy Rosary, we contemplate the face of man and woman, called to life in Christ. We bring to our praying of the Rosary everything which makes up our life, all of which Christ desires to take up with us, to unite to the mystery of His suffering, dying and rising from the dead. Through the praying of the Rosary, we contemplate the Face of Christ and, thereby, discover the deepest truth about ourselves.

---

[79] John Paul II, "Rosarium Virginis Mariae," 23.
[80] cf. Luke 2:35; John Paul II, "Rosarium Virginis Mariae," 24.
[81] John Paul II, "Rosarium Virginis Mariae," 25.

HOW TO PRAY *the* HOLY ROSARY

1. Make the Sign of the Cross.
2. Pray the Apostles' Creed while holding the crucifix.
3. Pray the Our Father on the first bead.
4. Pray one Hail Mary on each of the next three beads.
5. Pray the Glory Be on the final bead before the decades.
6. Announce the Mystery at the beginning of the decade.
7. Pray the Our Father.
8. Pray ten Hail Marys on each bead of the decade while meditating on the Mystery.
9. Pray the Glory Be on the bead between the decades.
10. Pray the Fatima Prayer on the same bead.
11. Pray the Hail, Holy Queen at the conclusion of the Holy Rosary.
12. Pray the concluding Prayer

PRAYERS *of the* HOLY ROSARY

THE APOSTLES' CREED

I believe in God, the Father almighty,
Creator of heaven and earth,
and in Jesus Christ, his only Son, our Lord,
who was conceived by the Holy Spirit,
born of the Virgin Mary,
suffered under Pontius Pilate,
was crucified, died and was buried;
he descended into hell;
on the third day he rose again from the dead;
he ascended into heaven,
and is seated at the right hand of God the Father almighty;
from there he will come to judge the living and the dead.

I believe in the Holy Spirit,
the holy catholic Church,
the communion of saints,
the forgiveness of sins,
the resurrection of the body,
and life everlasting.
Amen.

THE OUR FATHER
Our Father, who art in heaven,
hallowed be thy name;
thy kingdom come;
thy will be done on earth as it is in heaven.
Give us this day our daily bread;
and forgive us our trespasses
as we forgive those who trespass
against us;
and lead us not into temptation,
but deliver us from evil.
Amen.

THE HAIL MARY
Hail Mary, full of grace, the Lord is with you;
blessed are you among women,
and blessed is the fruit of your womb, Jesus.
Holy Mary, Mother of God,
pray for us sinners
now and at the hour of our death.
Amen.

THE GLORY BE (*The* Doxology)
Glory be to the Father, the Son, and the Holy Spirit;
as it was in the beginning, is now, and ever shall be,
world without end. Amen.

THE FATIMA PRAYER
O my Jesus, forgive us our sins, save us from the fires of hell; lead all souls to Heaven, especially those who have most need of your mercy.

THE HAIL HOLY QUEEN

Hail, holy Queen, mother of mercy,
our life, our sweetness, and our hope.
To you we cry, poor banished children of Eve;
to you we send up our sighs,
mourning and weeping in this valley of tears.
Turn, then, most gracious advocate,
your eyes of mercy toward us;
and after this, our exile,
show unto us the blessed fruit of your womb, Jesus.
O clement, O loving, O sweet Virgin Mary.

V. Pray for us, O holy Mother of God.

R. That we may be made worthy of the promises of Christ.

Let us pray: O God, whose Only Begotten Son, by his life, Death, and Resurrection, has purchased for us the rewards of eternal life, grant, we beseech thee, that while meditating on these mysteries of the most holy Rosary of the Blessed Virgin Mary, we may imitate what they contain and obtain what they promise, through the same Christ our Lord. Amen.

MYSTERIES *of the* HOLY ROSARY

THE JOYFUL MYSTERIES

(Mondays, Saturdays, the Sundays of Advent, and Sundays from Epiphany until Lent)

1. The Annunciation of the Angel Gabriel to Mary
   (Luke 1:26-38)
2. The Visitation of Mary to Elizabeth
   (Luke 1:39-56)
3. The Birth of Our Lord
   (Luke 2:1-20)
4. The Presentation of the Infant Jesus in the Temple
   (Luke 2:22-39)
5. The Finding of the Child Jesus in the Temple
   (Luke 2:41-52)

THE LUMINOUS MYSTERIES

(Thursdays)

1. The Baptism of Jesus in the Jordan River
   (Matthew 3:13-17)
2. The Wedding Feast at Cana
   (John 2:1-11)
3. The Proclamation of the Kingdom of God
   (Mark 1:15, 2:3-12, Luke 7:47-48)
4. The Transfiguration of Jesus
   (Matthew 17:1-8)
5. The Institution of the Eucharist
   (Matthew 26:26-29)

THE SORROWFUL MYSTERIES

(Tuesdays, Fridays, and daily from Ash Wednesday until Easter Sunday)

1. The Agony of Jesus in the Garden
   (Luke 22:39-46)
2. The Scourging at the Pillar
   (Mark 15:6-15)
3. The Crowning with Thorns
   (Matthew 27:28-31)
4. The Carrying of the Cross
   (Luke 23:26-32)
5. The Crucifixion
   (John 19:17-24)

THE GLORIOUS MYSTERIES

(Wednesdays, and the Sundays from Easter until Advent)

1. The Resurrection of Jesus
   (Matthew 28:1-10)
2. The Ascension of Jesus
   (Acts 1:6-11)
3. The Descent of the Holy Spirit at Pentecost
   (Acts 2:1-13)
4. The Assumption of Mary into Heaven
   (Revelation 11:19-12:1)
5. The Coronation of Mary as Queen of Heaven and Earth
   (Revelation 12:1)

LITANY *of the* SACRED HEART

Leader: Lord, have mercy.
R/. Christ, have mercy.

Leader: Lord, have mercy. Christ, hear us.
R/. Christ, graciously hear us.

Leader: God, the Father of Heaven,
R/. have mercy on us.

Leader: God the Son, Redeemer of the world,
R/. have mercy on us.

Leader: God the Holy Spirit,
R/. have mercy on us.

Holy Trinity, one God,
R/. have mercy on us.

Heart of Jesus, Son of the eternal Father, **R/.**
Heart of Jesus, formed by the Holy Spirit in the womb of the Virgin Mother, **R/.**
Heart of Jesus, substantially united to the Word of God, **R/.**
Heart of Jesus, of infinite majesty, **R/.**
Heart of Jesus, sacred temple of God, **R/.**
Heart of Jesus, tabernacle of the Most High, **R/.**
Heart of Jesus, house of God and gate of Heaven, **R/.**
Heart of Jesus, burning furnace of charity, **R/.**
Heart of Jesus, abode of justice and love, **R/.**
Heart of Jesus, full of goodness and love, **R/.**
Heart of Jesus, abyss of all virtues, **R/.**
Heart of Jesus, most worthy of all praise, **R/.**
Heart of Jesus, King and center of all hearts, **R/.**
Heart of Jesus, in Whom are all the treasures of wisdom and knowledge, **R/.**

Heart of Jesus, in Whom dwells the fullness of divinity, **R/.**
Heart of Jesus, in Whom the Father was well pleased, **R/.**
Heart of Jesus, of Whose fullness we have all received, **R/.**
Heart of Jesus, desire of the everlasting hills, **R/.**
Heart of Jesus, patient and most merciful, **R/.**
Heart of Jesus, enriching all who invoke Thee, **R/.**
Heart of Jesus, fountain of life and holiness, **R/.**
Heart of Jesus, propitiation for our sins, **R/.**
Heart of Jesus, loaded down with opprobrium, **R/.**
Heart of Jesus, bruised for our offenses, **R/.**
Heart of Jesus, obedient unto death, **R/.**
Heart of Jesus, pierced with a lance, **R/.**
Heart of Jesus, source of all consolation, **R/.**
Heart of Jesus, our life and resurrection, **R/.**
Heart of Jesus, our peace and reconciliation, **R/.**
Heart of Jesus, victim for sin, **R/.**
Heart of Jesus, salvation of those who trust in Thee, **R/.**
Heart of Jesus, hope of those who die in Thee, **R/.**
Heart of Jesus, delight of all the saints, **R/.**

Leader: Lamb of God, Who takes away the sins of the world,
R/. spare us, O Lord.

Leader: Lamb of God, Who takes away the sins of the world,
R/. graciously hear us, O Lord.

Leader: Lamb of God, Who takes away the sins of the world,
R/. have mercy on us.

Leader: Jesus, meek and humble of Heart,
R/. make our hearts like unto Thine.

HYMNS

TO JESUS CHRIST, OUR SOV'REIGN KING

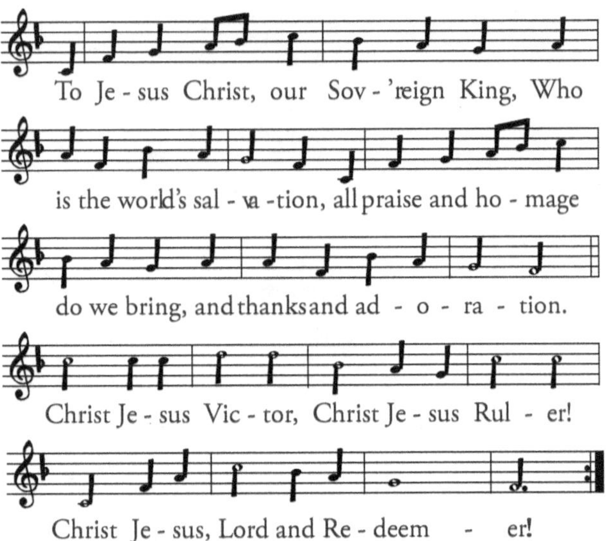

2. Thy reign extend, O King benign,
   To ev'ry land and nation,
   For in Thy kingdom, Lord divine,
   Alone we find salvation.
   Christ Jesus Victor,
   Christ Jesus Ruler!
   Christ Jesus, Lord and Redeemer!

3. To Thee and to Thy Church, great King,
   We pledge our hearts' oblation,
   Until before Thy throne we sing,
   In endless jubilation.
   Christ Jesus Victor,
   Christ Jesus Ruler!
   Christ Jesus, Lord and Redeemer!

4. Thy majesty shall be the praise
 And thanks of ev'ry nation,
 To thee the world with joy shall raise
 The voice of exultation.
 Christ Jesus Victor,
 Christ Jesus Ruler!
 Christ Jesus, Lord and Redeemer!

5. May God the Father, God the Son,
 And God the Spirit bless us!
 Let all the world praise him alone,
 Let solemn awe possess us.
 Christ Jesus Victor,
 Christ Jesus Ruler!
 Christ Jesus, Lord and Redeemer!

HOLY GOD, WE PRAISE THY NAME

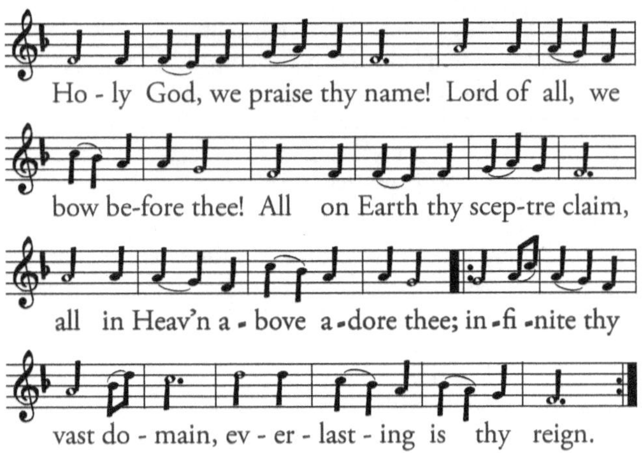

2. Hark! the loud celestial hymn
   Angel choirs above are raising!
   Cherubim and seraphim,
   In unceasing chorus praising,
   Fill the heav'ns with sweet accord;
   Holy, holy, holy, Lord!

3. Lo! The blessed Twelve proclaim
   To the Father hymns of glory;
   Prophets sing in loud acclaim;
   Martyrs tell the wondrous story;
   And from morn to set of sun
   Through the Church they sing as one.

4. Holy Father, Holy Son,
   Holy Spirit, Three we name thee,
   While in essence only One,
   Undivided God we claim thee;
   And adoring bend the knee,
   While we own the mystery.

IMMACULATE MARY

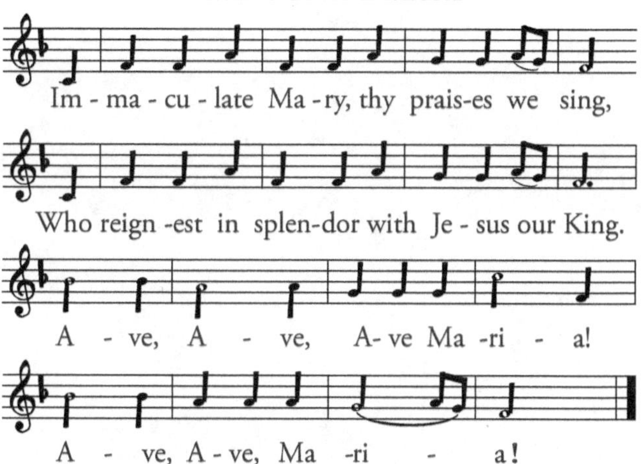

2. In heaven the blessed thy glory proclaim,
On earth we thy children invoke thy fair name.
Ave, Ave, Ave María! Ave, Ave María!

3. Thy name is our power, thy virtues our light,
Thy love is our comfort, thy pleading our might.
Ave, Ave, Ave, María! Ave, Ave, María!

4. We pray for our Mother, the Church upon earth,
And bless, sweetest Lady, the land of our birth.
Ave, Ave, Ave Maria! Ave, Ave Maria!

Sources / Acknowledgments

Alacoque, Margaret Mary. *The Autobiography of St. Margaret Mary*. TAN, 1986.

The Adoremus Hymnal. San Francisco: Ignatius Press, 1997. Used with permission. Immaculate Mary, Hymn #532
To Jesus Christ, Our Sov'reign King, Hymn #480 Holy God, We Praise Thy Name, Hymn #461

Catechism of the Catholic Church. Washington, D.C.: United States Catholic Conference, Inc., 1994.

Crawley-Boevey, Mateo. *Jesus King of Love*. Brewster, MA: Paraclete Press, 1997.

Diocese of La Crosse. *The Enthronement of the Sacred Heart Ceremonial for the Family*. La Crosse, WI: Office of Sacred Worship, 2003.

Paul II, John. 2002. "Rosarium Virginis Mariae on the Most Holy Rosary (October 16, 2002) | John Paul II." Www.vatican.va. 2002. https://www.vatican.va/content/john-paul-ii/en/apost_letters/2002/documents/hf_jp-ii_apl_20021016_rosarium-virginis-mariae.html.

Larkin, Francis. *Enthronement of the Sacred Heart*. National Sacred Heart Enthronement Center, 2009.

O'Donnell, Timothy T. *Heart of the Redeemer.* Manassas, VA: Trinity Communications, 1989; reprint, San Francisco: Ignatius Press, 1992.

Litany of the Sacred Heart of Jesus. Copyright © 2009 Dominican Sisters of Saint Cecilia. Used with permission.

Sacred Heart of Jesus oil painting used throughout this document was produced by an unknown artist. The original oil painting hangs in the Archbishop's Residence in Saint Louis, Missouri.

Sacred Scripture quotations taken from the *Revised Standard Version Catholic* Edition of the Holy Bible.

Verheylezoon, Louis. *Devotion to the Sacred Heart.* Westminster, MD: The Newman Press, 1955.

Certificates of Enthronement

Those who have completed the Enthronement of the Sacred Heart of Jesus in their home, parish, school, or other setting are invited to obtain a Certificate of Enthronement as a spiritual remembrance of this act of consecration. By typing the URL into your browser or scanning the QR code provided below, readers will be directed to a webpage where certificates may be downloaded and printed.

The Church rejoices in every act by which Christ is welcomed and honored as King. May this certificate serve as a sign of gratitude and encouragement, and may the Sacred Heart of Jesus continue to bless all who entrust themselves, their families, and their communities to His loving reign.

To download Certificates of Enthronement, type into your browser:

mariancatechist.com/enthronement-certificates

or

Scan and Download Certificates of Enthronement

SECUNDUM COR TUUM

Make a pilgrimage to the Shrine of Our Lady of Guadalupe.

guadalupeshrine.org

Are you called to become a Marian Catechist? Find out at:

mariancatechist.com

cardinalburke.com

www.ingramcontent.com/pod-product-compliance
Lightning Source LLC
La Vergne TN
LVHW091145080826
845145LV00008B/2264

* 9 7 8 1 9 6 3 7 1 6 0 1 6 *